**ASPATORE
BOOKS**

About Aspatore Books
Business Intelligence From Industry Insiders
www.Aspatore.com

Aspatore Books publishes only the biggest names in the business world, including C-level (CEO, CTO, CFO, COO, CMO, Partner) leaders from over half the world's 500 largest companies and other leading executives. Aspatore Books publishes the Inside the Minds, Bigwig Briefs, ExecEnablers and Aspatore Business Review imprints in addition to other best selling business books and journals. By focusing on publishing only the biggest name executives, Aspatore Books provides readers with proven business intelligence from industry insiders, rather than relying on the knowledge of unknown authors and analysts. Aspatore Books focuses on publishing traditional print books, while our portfolio company, Big Brand Books focuses on developing areas within the book-publishing world. Aspatore Books is committed to providing our readers, authors, bookstores, distributors and customers with the highest quality books, book related services, and publishing execution available anywhere in the world.

The *Inside the Minds* Series
Real World Intelligence From Industry Insiders
www.InsideTheMinds.com

Inside the Minds was conceived in order to give readers actual insights into the leading minds of business executives worldwide. Because so few books or other publications are actually written by executives in industry, *Inside the Minds* presents an unprecedented look at various industries and professions never before available. Each chapter is comparable to a white paper and is a very future oriented look at where their industry/profession is heading. In addition, the *Inside the Minds* web site makes the reading experience interactive by enabling readers to post messages and interact with each other, become a reviewer for upcoming books, read expanded comments on the topics covered and nominate individuals for upcoming books. The *Inside the Minds* series is revolutionizing the business book market by publishing an unparalleled group of executives and providing an unprecedented introspective look into the leading minds of the business world.

About Big Brand Books

Big Brand Books assists leading companies and select individuals with book writing, publisher negotiations, book publishing, book sponsorship, worldwide book promotion and generating a new revenue stream from publishing. Services also include white paper, briefing, research report, bulletin, newsletter and article writing, editing, marketing and distribution. The goal of Big Brand Books is to help our clients capture the attention of prospective customers, retain loyal clients and penetrate new target markets by sharing valuable information in publications and providing the highest quality content for readers worldwide. For more information please visit www.BigBrandBooks.com or email jonp@bigbrandbooks.com.

INSIDE THE MINDS

INSIDE THE MINDS:
Leading Marketers

*Industry Leaders Share Their Knowledge on the
Future of Marketing, Advertising and
Building Successful Brands*

**ASPATORE
BOOKS**

Published by Aspatore Books, Inc.
For information on bulk orders, sponsorship opportunities or any other questions please email store@aspatore.com. For corrections, company/title updates, comments or any other inquiries please email info@aspatore.com.

First Printing, October 2001
10 9 8 7 6 5 4 3 2 1

ISBN 1-58762-053-7

Library of Congress Card Number: 2001118201

Cover design by Michael Lepera/Ariosto Graphics & James Weinberg

Material in this book is for educational purposes only. This book is sold with the understanding that neither any of the authors or the publisher is engaged in rendering legal, accounting, investment, or any other professional service.

This book is printed on acid free paper.

A special thanks to all the individuals that made this book possible.

Special thanks also to: Jo Alice Hughes, Rinad Beidas, Kirsten Catanzano, Melissa Conradi and especially Ted Juliano

The views expressed by the individuals in this book do not necessarily reflect the views shared by the companies they are employed by (or the companies mentioned in this book). The companies referenced may not be the same company that the individual works for since the publishing of this book.

ASPATORE MARKETING REVIEW
Tear Out This Page and Mail or Fax To:

Aspatore Books, PO Box 883, Bedford, MA 01730
Or Fax To (617) 249-1970

Name:

Email:

Shipping Address:

City: State: Zip:

Billing Address:

City: State: Zip:

Phone:

Lock in at the Current Rates Today-Rates Increase Every Year
Please Check the Desired Length Subscription:

1 Year ($1,090) _____   2 Years (Save 10%-$1,962) _____
5 Years (Save 20%-$4,360) _____   10 Years (Save 30%-$7,630) _____
Lifetime Subscription ($24,980) _____

(If mailing in a check you can skip this section but please read fine print below and sign below)
Credit Card Type (Visa & Mastercard & Amex):

Credit Card Number:

Expiration Date:

Signature:

Would you like us to automatically bill your credit card at the end of your subscription so there is no discontinuity in service? (You can still cancel your subscription at any point before the renewal date.) Please circle: Yes   No

*(Please note the billing address much match the address on file with your credit card company exactly)

Terms & Conditions - We shall send a confirmation receipt to your email address. If ordering from Massachusetts, please add 5% sales tax on the order (not including shipping and handling). If ordering from outside of the US, an additional $51.95 per year will be charged for shipping and handling costs. All issues are paperback and will be shipped as soon as they become available. Sorry, no returns or refunds at any point unless automatic billing is selected, at which point you may cancel at any time before your subscription is renewed (no funds shall be returned however for the period currently subscribed to). Issues that are not already published will be shipped upon publication date. Publication dates are subject to delay-please allow 1-2 weeks for delivery of first issue. If a new issue is not coming out for another month, the issue from the previous quarter will be sent for the first issue. For the most up to date information on publication dates and availability please visit www.Aspatore.com.

Inside the Minds:
Leading Marketers

*Industry Leaders Share Their Knowledge on the
Future of Marketing, Advertising and
Building Successful Brands*

Contents

CONNECTING WITH CONSUMER NEEDS

STEPHEN C. JONES

The Coca-Cola Company

Chief Marketing Officer

Enjoyable Aspects of Marketing

Think of marketing as a series of processes. You begin by assembling qualitative and quantitative data. Second, you convert that data into useful insight. Third, you use those insights as a foundation to build a coherent marketing strategy. You create your plans and then executive that strategy in the marketplace. I've always enjoyed the process of creating new ideas for consumers to engage in the brand life. It's the most dynamic process.

The second part of marketing that is fun is the leadership – pulling together people who really understand what we are all trying to achieve to create a collaborative network that can produce results. I hope to be recognized for bringing together the right people, figuring out the idea that we are going to pursue, and helping them make it happen. To me, that's where the fun comes from – allowing other people to be successful.

Biggest Challenges

Probably the biggest challenge is ensuring that you never lose the sense of excitement that makes marketing work. Having the insight into what people want and how they want it is one of the biggest challenges all marketers face.

With a brand like Coca-Cola, you have to be as much at the leading edge of innovation and contemporary communication as a start-up brand. Our challenge is to understand the changing mindset, needs, motivations, and aspirations of our consumers.

A brand like Coke has integrity that has been developed over 115 years. It has evolved, and it has become richer and more robust, but at its core are a set of broadly appealing, timeless values. Essentially, Coke has stood for something, and continues to stand for something. That's important. Maintaining that integrity while balancing it with contemporary lifestyles is one of our most exciting challenges.

We have been successful in the past by taking the brand into a market and really creating the "world of Coca-Cola"

– all those values, aspirations, attributes, and different kinds of things, which the brand stands for, and which people want to buy into. We invite people to be a part of the world of Coke. That was very successful for 115 years. In the last couple of years, possibly because technology has changed and empowered people with information, people are becoming more selective and don't rely as much on brands to define who they are.

Consequently, the Coca-Cola brand has changed its model, from inviting people into Coke's world, to focusing on understanding our consumers and making sure Coke fits into their world. Our shift in approach reflects a fundamental shift in our thinking. We used to talk about the brand as Coca-Cola's key asset. Now we view the quality of the relationship between people and our brand as our most important asset. We are determined to continuously renew and refresh that relationship on a day-to-day basis. We want to keep the contemporary expression of the brand very relevant. This is the key to success, and probably one of the greatest challenges that we have everywhere in the world.

One of the things that make it more interesting for us than others is the global nature of our brand. I heard (Former United States Ambassador to the U.N.) Richard Holbrook speak recently, and he said, "Coke is in more countries than the United Nations is." I couldn't quite figure out how we did that, but it's a fact! We have a brand that at its very core stands for the same thing in every country. We cannot change the architecture or positioning of the brand from country to country. At the same time we must understand people's needs, motivations, and behavior in every country, and we must ensure that we communicate with consumers in ways that resonate with them.

Creating Ties With Consumers and Then Connecting With Them

The process of gaining insight has to be very local. It would be a mistake to try to centralize the process of connecting with consumers. You have to have the best quality people who are well trained out in the marketplace, talking to people. This isn't just traditional qualitative and quantitative research methodology that I am talking about; I am talking about marketers who are on the street, in people's homes, and living in the community, so that they really understand the rhythms and nuances of daily life. We have a community of marketers around the world, each with a deep understanding of his or her own market, and each of whom is responsible for getting that insight. We can provide them with thought models and techniques and protocol on how to go get insight, but we leave it to them to detect trends and then translate them into opportunities around which we build our initiatives. I don't do that personally; I rely on marketers around the world to do that.

Connecting with people happens in a number of ways. The connection starts by making sure that the product you have is one people want and need and that it is a great product. Coca-Cola is a great-tasting, refreshing, thirst-quenching beverage that can't be copied. It has a unique flavor. It's absolutely dependable. You can trust in the product. That's essential in order to make the first connection.

We also connect through the positioning of the brand and the core values. Coke is about much more than quenching one's thirst; it's about a magical refreshment of one's body, mind, and spirit. There are certain things that the brand stands for. It is very alive. We need to connect with people through activities that are very alive. We choose to associate with sports, entertainment, and music because those are things that people are passionate about, and those are also things that can connect with the core values of the brand.

We connect with people on a day-to-day basis by ensuring that we are available to them as they go through their daily lives. We are determined to be everywhere people are going to be. The connections are made through advertising communications and promotions. We are changing the way we promote – moving away from a concentration on the big wins and sweepstakes and toward a greater focus on becoming more relevant to consumers on a day-to-day basis. We want to make a daily connection with Coke's consumers – in a way that is relevant in their lives.

Favorite Marketing Tools

We use a number of interesting marketing tools, from TV advertising, which The Coca-Cola Company pioneered at the dawn of the television age, to stimulating trial through coupons. Both are mass marketing tools. To me the more exciting tools are the new methods of creating unique and personal one-on-one relationships. For instance, online interactive programs via the Internet allow us to communicate with individuals of like attitudes and not only send messages one way, but be truly interactive and responsive. We're positioning "Life Tastes Good" for certain youth-attitude segments online very differently and in ways that each segment understands and desires. A related tool that is becoming far more important is data-based marketing. We're having thousands of "conversations" with consumers every day and are now able to affordably record their email addresses and return to them with unique offers.

The real goal of Coke is to make sure that we appeal to young people, and that the brand becomes part of their lives. No matter what the media – online or offline – communication is key. How are you dialoguing and interacting with these young people? I don't think the major tool is TV; increasingly it's online interactiveness and being involved in their games and activities. That's one of the most fascinating areas – making sure we are relevant to 13-year-olds who are about to make decisions for themselves about what brands they are going to use for the rest of their lives. You can't just use TV anymore; you actually have to initiate a dialogue with them. That's the most exciting and dynamic new tool that we have available to us.

We are at the earliest stages of understanding how to utilize computer games and Internet chat rooms. Everybody explored the billboard. Some people tried putting traditional film on, but it didn't work terribly well. It wasn't relevant to young people in that medium. There is a continuous set of experiments going on, and I think that's one of the most interesting areas right now.

What Constitutes a Successful Marketing Campaign

Success is largely determined by the objectives you set for yourself at the beginning. However, while achieving the goal is very important, the way in which you get there – the creativity, innovativeness, leadership, substance, and value created – promises longer-term benefits than those derived from simply achieving those short-term goals. If you can achieve your basic, fundamental objectives and goals and do it in a way that creates long-term relationships with people, where people are prepared to make a commitment back to a brand, then that is really true success.

There is another one. It isn't about the consumer; it is about the people who work on the brands. When people who put the stuff together, whether they are financial managers, salesmen, or brand managers, when they feel they have done something worthwhile and improved the state of somebody's life or the quality of the company, then that is another measure of success.

How Marketing Drives the Company

Marketing very much drives the company. Our business is making and selling beverages. But within that business of being a total beverage company, the most effective tool we have is marketing. There is no question that marketing drives the understanding into people's needs, the creation of the brand portfolio, and the ideas that people rally around. The financial people do things as an outflow of the things that the marketing sales operation community does. To me, it is very much the driver. It is normally the place where the ideas are generated, and where you will find the architects of the portfolio. As we look at the new Coca-Cola Company, which is emerging as a total beverage company, its architects were – in large measure – the marketers.

It is essential to make sure that everyone, no matter what their discipline is, feels they are a part of the marketing operation and are contributing important ideas and creating outcomes that are important for the company. Everyone is involved in bringing marketing to life no matter what their discipline.

Reinventing Brands to Stay Fresh

A brand has an essential integrity and a character it has built over time. You have to maintain that integrity. For Coke, that integrity exists in a number of places. Coca-Cola is authentic and original and is the "real thing." It has a sense of brightness, excitement, fun, and being alive, and through the 115 years, we have done things that have built up those characteristics of the brand. These are the timeless values that reside at the core of the brand.

Every day we have to contemporize the expression of that. Given the rapid pace of change in today's world, it's a challenge that gets bigger every year. The way we connect with people must be reinvented on an ongoing basis, but the essence of the core never changes. Coke is a brand with timeless qualities.

Changes in the Ease of Marketing and Changes in Marketing Over the Next Five Years

I have lived most of the last couple of years in Japan. There is a hyper-competitiveness there. The beverage industry is in a state of continuous change. Japan has more than 7,000 beverage brands, and about 1,500 new ones are introduced every single year. In markets like Japan, consumer needs are constantly changing; the competitive landscape is constantly changing; and you must be able to go to market at hyper speed. That is exhilarating.

But it's not just Japan. The pace of change throughout the world is accelerating. We've seen more changes in the past five years than we saw in the last 20 years. In the next five years, we will see double or triple the changes we saw in the last five years. That is going to be very challenging to keep up with that pace.

As this company reinvents itself from being The Coca-Cola Company, which sells just Coca-Cola, to The Coca-Cola Company, which is a total beverage company, we encounter a number of challenges: understanding the full range of people's needs; developing the portfolio and route to market that they want; and having the right innovations, packaging, and product design. That's what is going to make it more interesting, because competitiveness and consumer needs are going to change ever faster.

As people change, marketing will change. Marketing is simply a way to connect the brands with people. It will change in the world of media. The media world is fragmenting, and it will continue to fragment. People will be able to access information in so many different ways, and we as marketers will be able to reach people in so many different ways. Our messaging needs to become far more interactive and individual as opposed to mass marketing.

Selling Your Product and Vision

You must sell your product and your vision internally and externally. Let's start with internally, because the internal audience is very important. We reach our own people in a number of ways. We talk openly and online with one another. We frequently gather together as a community. Among the most important tools in getting people to understand a vision is consistency. A consistent vision will lift their spirits by giving them something that they believe is strategically sound and inspirational. Keeping it consistent, new, and fresh is so important. If we can do that, then not only does the community understand what we are doing, but each individual also feels that he or she is a part of it. By understanding it and feeling a part of it, each individual feels responsible for it and can add to it and build on it. This is one of the most important elements of leadership. That kind of buy-in leads to more imaginative programs than any one manager could devise.

How do we communicate our vision to the public? The way in which we do that is really by being very inclusive with people and very overt and open about the brand. People believe they own Coca-Cola, and it's not ours; it's theirs.

It's as much their vision about what the brand needs to be as it is ours. We have to steer it, no question. There are only certain corridors that the public will accept us taking our vision to. We have to be mindful of that. We don't always have to stay inside them, but we have to be careful about our communication to people if we are going to take it outside of that realm. As long as we have talked to them and understand how they are going to react to it, normally we are pretty successful.

To sustain our vision of the brand, we must communicate it, and we must live it. By communicating it, I mean going through some very complex insight development and science to understand how people think and make decisions. There is a complex set of fairly important things that you have to do to create insight. To me, crystallizing that down to the simplest form in a couple of sentences is the key to success. You must be able to state the vision in a way that anybody can understand what it is you're talking about. The public must see our vision in everything that we do and we must make it extremely easy for them to see it – not only on TV, but also on the street and in their schools, offices, and communities.

We actually have a fairly active Web site. A lot of people like to visit www.coca-cola.com because it is fairly open about what the brand is, what it stands for, what it offers, and what value it can add to your life. People really appreciate that.

Managing During Turbulent Times

First of all, it's like living in a fishbowl with everybody watching what you do every day. We very clearly believe that we have the right strategy and are on track to deliver it. I try not to look at the newspapers and read the clippings so that I don't worry about what the analysts, reporters, and pundits are saying. I think continuously about what the consumer is thinking about. We are the ones who are responsible for deciding where to take the company, and we will take it there. If you believe you are on the right course, which is driven by your insight into what consumers want, you can resist the temptation to become distracted by the second-guessing.

We know what we need to do to perform. We believe that the strategies that we are following are the right ones. The key is remaining calm, acting quickly and flexibly, and being determined to follow the course we have picked. We are not going to deviate from it, unless the time comes when new information indicates that there is a better, more effective course to follow.

Becoming a Marketing Leader

You need huge confidence and a clear picture of where you want to go. You must be able to communicate your vision to everybody in an inspirational way and then empower and inspire others to build on the ideas and execute them. That's what leadership is all about. In this world if you do not have incredible confidence and a really clear picture of what you want the world to become (the part of world you are involved in), you can't lead. Unless you are able to communicate that, you can't lead.

A leader must be creative and must create new ideas and paths. That's a very important part of leadership and distinguishes great leaders from good managers. Great leaders see the ideas – whether they are their own or the ideas of others – and are determined to pursue them with vigor. They have conviction. And they have confidence to liberate the troops to perform. A leader draws people into ideas and keeps the goals clearly in front of them, nurtures the thinkers and doers together, and consistently makes the right decision in a simple, transparent manner.

I have always credited Woody Allen for saying that "90 percent of success is just showing up." I remember 1994-95, when the Asian economy collapsed. There was no manual, no economist who was going to tell us what could happen three days or years from then. Nobody had a clue. It was a great relief to be able to go to the team every single day and acknowledge that life is unpredictable, and that all we can do is test things. One of the most important things we did was to rally round each other. We became very expressive about how we felt about what was going on. That helped people continuously "show up" and work through the solutions.

Successful people create certain rules about behavior with one another. It has to do with listening, continuous data mining, listening to the consumer, and talking to retailers and business partners. I find that in a period where there is great stress in the marketplace, the more you listen and have a set of rules around, the more successful and faster you will create the successful solution.

In a time of market crisis, it is crucial to be open to any idea, remain flexible, and be supportive. It is easy in a crisis to blame other people for what is going on. You need a set of rules where you are supportive, meet more often, and communicate, because this is the only way to get through it. A leader builds confidence by telling people what he or she is thinking and feeling – almost becoming a little vulnerable and more open than normal. When you become more vulnerable, people become more a part of what you are and share more with you. The leadership team in times of crisis has to take accountability for the relationships with the people they are working with and for understanding what is going on in the marketplace.

Keeping Your Edge and Setting Goals

I have my favorite newspapers that I read on a regular basis, which are a selection from around the world. I love to listen to the results of focus groups from around the world. I love to travel and be in the marketplace. Recently I went to Germany, a market that has been difficult for us as of late. I went with one other person. We had three days to go in and assess the situation. The traditional way to do that is to go into the boardrooms, sit down with the local business people, hear them make presentations, assess the situation, and design a course of action.

To stay on the edge you can't do that; you have to be on the street. Life, creativity, and strategy are on the street. You keep your edge by being on the street and seeing what is going on with the people. When we travel, my group is not about boardrooms and meetings; we are about seeing what people want and testing ideas by talking with people on the street. Then we brainstorm afterward as to what the best thing is and try to come up with the best idea.

We have enjoyed a prominent position in the minds of consumers, and as a result we have high expectations for ourselves – as does Wall Street. We will always maintain that high standard, whether it is PE ratio of 40:45 or esteem or a goal of leadership. We will do things that other people won't think about, whether they are social, environmental, or whatever other area. We have a traditional set of quantitative volume profit type of goals, which we set, to ensure that we achieve our high standards of income, PE ratio, and market capital.

Then we have a set of goals around corporate leadership. Those are set collectively. (Chairman and CEO) Doug Daft is a great leader in terms of establishing commitment to a wide range of community areas of interest and setting specific goals within areas. Those are done collaboratively, and then they are discussed an awful lot. We get together once a month. Those softer goals are in a continuous state of flux and evolution, driven by what people are discovering as they try to become better leaders and community people. To that end, The Coca-Cola Company has a collaborative culture up and down through the ranks of the organization.

Skills Needed on the Marketing Team

We want the same thing everybody else does; we just want more, better, and faster. First of all, I think every company has a different culture and attracts a certain type of person. At Coke, culture is fairly strong. We want people to be a part of the culture.

Second, we want a lot of diversity – a lot of people with a lot of different ideas who can approach things from different directions. There is never just one solution. Diversity of thinking is critical in the type of people we are looking for.

In addition to people who will become part of our culture and add to the diversity of that culture, we want skills. We want really bright people who are terribly ambitious about making success happen – not just for themselves, but also for the team and company around them. They need to be curious and inventive and driven in an incredibly fast-paced, complex world.

Finally, we want people who want to make things happen fast, who aren't afraid to execute, who take action on good ideas. Those are the people we need to build a team around the world.

Golden Rules of Marketing

Consumers are at the center of everything we do. Everything we own in the brand is essential to maintain our commitment to the quality, integrity, and values of the brand. In the end, people are making all their choices based on what that brand stands for. Make sure you are continuously investing in the core essence of what the brand stands for.

Trust, respect, commitment, and collaboration of the people who are designing the market – this must always be maintained at the highest level to get anything decent or creative executed.

Stephen C. Jones is the chief marketing officer of The Coca-Cola Company and is one of the key architects in the reinvention of The Coca-Cola Company. A native of Toronto, Mr. Jones joined Coca-Cola Canada in 1986 as brand manager for Sprite. In 1988, he moved to Coca-Cola USA in Atlanta, where he was responsible for the Diet Coke and Sprite brands in the U.S. In 1990, he was named marketing manager for Coca-Cola Great Britain. He was promoted to region manager, Coca-Cola Great Britain Region in 1991.

In 1994, Mr. Jones became senior vice president, Consumer Marketing, for Coca-Cola (Japan) Co., Ltd. He progressed through a series of executive positions in Japan and was named deputy division manager and executive vice president in 1997 and headed the Coca-Cola (Japan) Co. Leadership Team from 1998. In 1999, Mr. Jones was appointed president and chief executive officer of The Minute Maid Company, an operating group of The Coca-Cola Company that is the world's leading producer and marketer of fruit beverages, with products in more than 75 countries.

In January 2000, Mr. Jones was named senior vice president and chief marketing officer for The Coca-Cola Company. In this role, he is responsible for the global marketing strategy for the Company. Prior to joining The Coca-Cola Company, Mr. Jones held brand management positions with Kimberly-Clark Canada from 1983 until 1986. From 1977 through 1983, he served in various assistant roles to politicians and senior government managers. Mr. Jones received his BA from the University of Toronto. He is married and has three children.

STAYING CUSTOMER-FOCUSED

T. MICHAEL GLENN

FedEx Corporation

Executive Vice President,

Market Development & Corporate Communications

Exciting Aspects of Marketing

What excites me most about marketing is getting feedback from customers saying they love our company, the services we provide, our employees, and our approach to the business. That feedback is really the culmination of all the efforts that go into marketing, whether it's product development, pricing, or promotion.

What excites me most about what we can do today is one-to-one marketing. Obviously individual customers have individual requirements, and the ability to understand those requirements using today's data-mining techniques allows companies to create mass customization of the value proposition. You can tweak the value proposition in a way that you know will meet the customer's requirements.

Equally important is how customers want to do business with you. They may want to call an 800 number to get basic package tracking information, or they may want the data pushed to them automatically, or they may want to go to our Web site or their wireless device to get information. Technology has changed the marketing field significantly. Whether you're talking about product promotion, product planning, or advertising, technology has really opened up the field, particularly in the interactive arena.

Most Important Elements of Marketing

To be successful in marketing, you have to develop your company's value proposition in a way that meets or exceeds the customer's requirements and expectations. You also must have a value delivery system that ensures your message breaks through. If you are successful, your company is going to meet the market's requirements. Marketing is not rocket science. It's more common sense than anything else, but it's amazing how many people don't have the ability to sit down and understand what customers are really looking for.

For example, look back at the dot-bombs. If those companies had had a clear understanding of what the consumer really wanted and made sure their value proposition was solid, they would have saved themselves a lot of time and money. Customers will always tell you if your product or service is going to work. Just listen to them. The rest is blocking and tackling.

Looking to the Consumer for What They Want

There is a cartoon that our chairman likes to quote. It's a Pogo cartoon, and Pogo's claim-to-fame leadership principle is to find a parade and jump in front of it. That's really what we try to do at FedEx. We try to stay in tune with our customers' needs and deliver the solution before anyone else can. In the case of the transition of our brand from Federal Express to FedEx, customers made the switch before we did. If they wanted to refer to us as FedEx, why try to stop them? This demonstrates that when you take the time to listen to your customers, they will tell you what they want. You have to be smart enough to listen, however, and then have the courage to act upon it.

Clear and Simple Marketing Messages

Research supports the fact that a customer can't remember much about a brand, especially if you're relying solely on advertising to communicate the key attributes of your brand. I can reel off several key attributes that set FedEx apart from our competition, but it is difficult to effectively convey them in a print ad, a 30-second commercial, a direct-marketing campaign, or a Web-based campaign. You have to develop two to three key messages that you want to leave with the customer, regardless of the medium used. And the key to developing those messages is understanding what motivates the customer to buy.

In the case of FedEx, our key message is reliability. Once customers start using us based on our reliability, a relationship is established with the customer. And from that established relationship, there is plenty of opportunity over time to communicate some or all of the key attributes that set us apart from the competition.

The Marketing Role in a Company

Marketing's primary role in any organization is to be the customer's advocate. There are always advocates in a company for cutting costs, operational issues, etc. However, the most important job for a marketing executive is to be the chief customer advocate – someone who is willing to fight for the customer at almost any cost. Doing battle on the customers' behalf may not always be pleasant, but I've found that what's in the best interest of the customer is usually in the best interest of the company.

By clearly understanding the needs of the customer and communicating them within the organization, the marketing executive can keep the value proposition fresh and the brand relevant.

Favorite Marketing Media

The best way to work with customers is in a one-on-one relationship. Nothing can take the place of an effective direct-selling relationship in finding, acquiring, and keeping customers. Fortunately, today, technology enables us to have a one-on-one relationship with the customer without having the personal contact typically seen in a sales environment.

Marketing Pitfalls

Over-promising is the one pitfall that a lot of companies fall into. There is an old saying that "great advertising is the best way to kill a bad product," simply because you over-promise. FedEx has been very careful to avoid over-promising by making sure that, as we go to market, we deliver upon the value proposition we have defined. A brand is only as good as the product or service it represents. The quickest way to tarnish our brand is to fail to deliver on our value proposition, which is absolute reliability. We protect against that at all costs.

The second pitfall is the inability to effectively communicate your value proposition and the essence of your brand. If you can't do this in a way that is relevant to the customer, you're in trouble.

Successful Marketing Campaigns

There is only one measure of success, and that is revenue growth. Your ability to attract, keep, and grow customers is the measure of success for any marketing organization. That's why we're in business. That's the key measure of success.

What You Need in a Marketing Team

You want a team that is energetic and passionate about delivering a value proposition and keeping it fresh. You want a team that clearly understands customer requirements and the market in general. It's also important to have a marketing organization that understands and knows how to use technology. Finally, you must have a team that can develop strategy and the tactics to support the strategy.

Effects of Killer Applications on Marketing

The killer applications are those that allow you to get closer to the customer. The ability to provide information to customers about a transaction, no matter where they are – office, car, home, or out of the country – is changing with newer technology. Research indicates that information about a package is just as important as the delivery of the package itself. Our ability to provide rich information about that transaction is an important part of our value proposition. When you understand broadband and wireless technologies and the avenues they open for a company like FedEx, you can get pretty excited.

For example, let's say a customer is shipping a package from the U.S. to Singapore. If we determine that the package is being held up in customs because the commercial invoice wasn't created properly, we can communicate with that customer proactively. This ability to proactively communicate with customers and solve problems while a package is en route helps us make their shipping experience with us more pleasurable.

The Internet and One-to-One Marketing

The major benefit of the Internet is that it allows you to create a richer one-to-one marketing relationship. For instance, through fedex.com, a customer can create preferences about the way they like to ship, the way they like to receive information, and which services they want to use. Capturing that type of information helps us better serve customers.

From information provided via fedex.com, we know a certain customer is going to ship a five-pound package every other Tuesday to Boise, Idaho. We've also learned that most of his or her international shipping is bound for Asia and Canada.

We now know something about that customer's business patterns. This information allows us to tailor our messages in a more meaningful way, so the customer is not constantly bombarded with irrelevant information. We can now deliver our value proposition to the customer through a very targeted channel, which enhances the customer's experience with our company.

All Employees Are Marketers

It's important to understand that everyone represents the brand and has an opportunity to make a positive or negative impact on the brand. In the case of our company, we may have a situation where we deliver a package late due to bad weather. If the courier walks in with a positive attitude and expresses apologies to the customer, the customer is more likely to accept the situation and appreciate the courier's commitment to delivering the package under adverse circumstances. On the other hand, if that courier comes in with a negative attitude because he is working in bad weather, that will have a negative impact on the customer.

Strategically, the chief executive must set the tone for any organization, especially a service organization. He or she must let it be known that in terms of the service experience nothing less than absolute customer delight can be accepted. This philosophy then filters down through the organization. On the other hand, if a CEO lets it be known that he is willing to sacrifice service to save money, that organization will find a lot of ways to cut corners on service.

Today's Marketing Challenges

I think today's market is more difficult in some respects and simpler in others. The number of media opportunities available to consumers today is certainly a challenge. Maybe you are an admirer of California condors. There is probably a magazine or Web site targeting condor lovers. With the customized media available today, reaching a broad audience in a cost effective way is very difficult.

At the same time, however, it is easier to gather information about the likes and dislikes of customers today, largely through database marketing. The one-to-one marketing possibilities available through the Internet allow you to customize your message, making it more effective and delivering a greater return on the investment.

Staying Customer-Connected

Talking with customers is the most important thing any marketing executive can do. There are a number of ways to do that, including attending customer forums, one-on-one contact, research, and looking at behavior data obtained through the Web. In addition to that, you have to be well read and current on the emerging trends, especially in technology. It helps to interact with your peers and to make sure that you are exchanging ideas with other companies in different industries that have similar issues. However, there can be no substitute for interacting with customers.

The Next Five Years in Marketing

I think it will be increasingly difficult to reach a broad audience in a cost-effective way, but we will be able to tailor our messages more effectively – and in a way that addresses specific needs of our customers. We've already made significant advances in that direction.

In the future, customers will not tolerate information that's not useful to them. There will be more resistance to generic forms of communication. Customers will expect us to understand their requirements and to address them with relevant advertising and promotion. Obviously technology is going to drive this change in a significant way.

In the past, if an infrequent FedEx customer wanted to use our services, they needed to fill out an airbill, and then call an 800 number to get a courier to come and pick up the package. Today, with the Internet, that can happen with a few clicks of a mouse. The customer can set preferences without making any contact with FedEx other than through electronic means. The ability to manage information through these new channels is going to make a significant difference in how we go to market and create new service solutions.

Keeping a Brand Fresh

Keeping a brand fresh is evolutionary, not revolutionary. A company has to understand the current and future requirements of the market it serves. As long as it does that, and maintains a value proposition that exceeds customers' needs, the brand will naturally evolve. Evolution means you change along with the market, albeit trying to stay ahead of where the market is going.

As it becomes increasingly difficult to market to larger and more diverse audiences, however, we've found that you can't rely on the strength of the brand alone to carry your messages. Smart marketers also use proactive corporate communications activities in concert with brand management. With a shared brand and corporate communications vision, we're able to speak with one voice to a multitude of audiences. This philosophy of one vision, one voice, yields far better results in terms of company positioning.

The Turning Point for FedEx as a Brand

The FedEx brand really began to take off in the late 1970s, when we began to take our message to a broader market, positioning FedEx as a problem-solver. Prior to that time our advertising focused on our networks, the number of planes, and the assets of the company. Our message was simply not getting through, however, because people were far less interested in how we did it, and much more interested in what we did.

So by positioning our company as a problem solver – and doing it in an engaging and humorous fashion – we changed the way people looked at FedEx. We re-focused the brand from one based on a physical network to a brand that became a common part of the everyday business language. With this change in our advertising approach, it was not long before people began to say they were going to "FedEx" a package.

Building a Brand in the Future

I believe building a mega-brand (like Coca-Cola or FedEx) is going to be more difficult in the future because of the proliferation and fragmentation of media outlets. Today, for instance, there are as many as 500 different TV channels. When FedEx started building its brand, there were just three major networks and PBS, so essentially, as an advertiser, you had a captive audience. The Internet was non-existent. From that perspective alone, today it's more difficult to build a brand. Amazon.com was able to do it by taking advantage of the Web hype and offering a good value proposition. A good value proposition, coupled with a good customer experience, is central to building a brand.

FedEx in the Future

I think the FedEx brand will continue to evolve as the markets we serve evolve. For example, as little as five years ago, FedEx offered only overnight, two-day, and three-day express services. Today, the FedEx brand encompasses a much broader portfolio of services. In addition to the express market, we provide efficient and reliable ground services and freight capabilities for shipments of virtually any size and shape. We also provide supply chain services to help companies maximize the productivity and efficiency of their operations, with solutions heavily tied to information technology. FedEx now serves more than 210 countries that represent over 98% of the world's GDP. So, as the markets we operate in change, FedEx changes. The challenge is to stay one or two steps ahead.

T. Michael Glenn is executive vice president of Market Development and Corporate Communications for FedEx Corporation, a $20 billion global transportation and logistics holding company. He is a member of the five-person Executive Committee, which is responsible for planning and executing the corporation's strategic business activities.

Glenn also serves as president and chief executive officer of FedEx Corporate Services Inc., responsible for all marketing, sales, and information technology functions for all FedEx Corporation operating companies.

Before FedEx Corporation was formed in January 1998, Glenn was senior vice president, Worldwide Marketing, Customer

Service, and Corporate Communications for FedEx, a position he held for five years. In that role, he was responsible for directing all marketing, customer service, employee communications, and public relations activities for the world's largest express transportation company.

After joining the Corporate Sales Department of FedEx in 1981, he was promoted to manager the following year. Glenn joined the Marketing Department in 1984 as managing director of Express Products Marketing and was promoted to vice president of North American marketing in 1985. Glenn became senior vice president, Catalog and Retail Services, in 1992.

Prior to joining FedEx, he worked in the Sales Division of the Dover Elevator Company. A native of Memphis, Tennessee, Glenn earned his bachelor's degree from the University of Mississippi and his MBA from The University of Memphis. Glenn currently serves on the board of directors for Youth Programs Inc. and the United Way. He also serves on the board of Community Commercial Bank.

BUILDING AN INTERNET MEGA-BRAND

KAREN EDWARDS

Yahoo!

Vice President, Brand Marketing

The Difference in Marketing for an Internet Company vs. a Brick and Mortar Company

Ironically, I think much of the success we have had at Yahoo! has been due to things that traditional companies do – understand the consumer, take the high road in communication, not get caught up in the latest product features (a practice that technology companies are sometimes guilty of). By focusing on the brand, we have needed to focus on the long term. I think in that regard, Yahoo! marketing is similar to that of traditional companies.

The difference between Yahoo! and traditional companies is we have two advantages. One is we have been able to ride the wave of the incredible phenomenon of the Internet. We understood the potential of the Internet to be a consumer technology. At the time, consumer-focused companies like America Online, CompuServe, and Prodigy were betting on closed, proprietary online services that didn't present the Internet in its full glory to consumers. Yahoo! was one of the few services that made the Internet easy to use and allowed people to explore beyond the boundaries of online services. Second, we took a page from the book of traditional leadership companies: We focused on owning the attributes of the category. For example, Tide isn't just Tide; it is the gold standard of laundry detergent. Everybody compares all other detergents to Tide because it stands for the cleanest laundry; it IS laundry detergent. Many can look at Yahoo! the same way. Rather than saying Yahoo! had this specific feature or benefit, we demonstrated that Yahoo! owned the overall attributes of the Internet category. The most important attributes to consumers were the ability to find any information, both practical and fun, and the ability to communicate with people. Eventually, it became clear that buying anything was also important, and so we expanded our communication to own that attribute as well. At the end of the day, we helped grow the category, perhaps as much as we grew Yahoo! This is not a new idea, but it works.

There are a few other aspects of our business that give us advantages over other traditional companies. One is that we have the ability to know and learn a tremendous amount of things about our users. From the very beginning, we were able to make decisions, which to some people may have looked as if we were just flying by the seat of our pants. But the reality was that we had access to information about our millions of users even back in 1996. We could look at their behavior, see what television shows were the most popular among them, and see other things that were important to our audience. We were able to alter our communication and marketing messages accordingly. Our production team was able to tailor our services to better meet user needs. We were able to do that very quickly, unlike the way a traditional manufacturer has to wait and see if a product is moving off the shelf before they can act upon that.

Building a Brand on a Budget

We've always worked with a smaller budget than many other companies that are brand focused. A lot of smaller brands have spent more money than we have. Our main competitors, AOL and Microsoft, have spent exponentially more than we have. However, we have been consistent, and there has been continuity throughout our short six-year history. We have also been able to extend and build our brand worldwide, not just in the United States. We are the #1, 2, or 3 brand in all the countries we operate in. In other countries where we don't operate a dedicated local service, we're still very well known.

How did we do it? I think that the emotional connection and the authenticity of Yahoo! have been the most important hooks. We thought long and hard about understanding what people liked and didn't like. And then we tried to convey and incorporate that into our brand and services and products so that users could see we could meet their needs. We looked at users, "near-surfers" (our name for people who were likely to adopt the technology), and non-users. The good news is that the Yahoo! product could and does deliver on the promises we made – that was key. It wouldn't have mattered how well we were reaching out to people if the product didn't deliver. We thought that the key thing was to give people emotional reasons to use Yahoo!, not just rational ones. In my mind, that is the essence of what a brand is – the emotional relationship you have with the consumer. Unfortunately, technology companies often have the idea that if you have the best technology and features, then people will find you and will try it ("if you build it, they will come"). My belief is that technology could be leap-frogged. I believed that any technological feature that we created could only last as an advantage as long as someone else didn't copy it. I always make the case that a brand is the one thing about a company that is absolutely impossible to emulate. Competitors may try to copy your brand, but they'll never be as authentic as the original. Any company that tries to copy your brand is making a fatal mistake; at best, they can only hope for second place. In this way, a brand is really the strongest differentiator there is. No one can take it away from you.

Does having a brand still matter as the category matures and there are fewer players? The penetration of the Internet right now is about 63 percent. Some would argue that the remainder may never get online. Some say we have reached a complete saturation point. I am a little bit more optimistic. When we first started going after people who weren't online yet, the conventional wisdom was that it would take a long time for the masses to come online. Clearly, it happened more quickly than most people imagined. We were focused on getting more than our fair share of these new users. And we did. The brand provided a "safe haven" for people who would have been otherwise reluctant to venture toward this new technology of the Internet.

Today, anyone who is still a holdout to the Internet phenomenon is going to go with the brands they know and therefore trust. So our brand helps separate Yahoo! from weaker companies as the inevitable consolidation occurs, and our industry matures. So today, our quest for market share focus is three-pronged: retain our leading share of loyal users, get more than our fair share of new users, and capture "switchers" from less-promising services.

Taking the Brand to the Next Level

At this point in Yahoo's lifecycle, taking our brand to the next level is about focusing on affinity and loyalty. Right now, we watch very closely to see who is using Yahoo!, why they use it, and what they do with it. That's the product experience relationship. We also look at their emotional relationship with the brand. We want to make sure that people continue to have a very strong emotional connection with Yahoo!. That can be tricky to manage through marketing alone. Sometimes, operational issues beyond our control or human mistakes – blackout, virus, hacker problem – can shape the perception that people have of Yahoo!. Hopefully, we can minimize these, and we do have a great brand and reputation that buys us some forgiveness. Yahoo! has evolved in many ways, yet has maintained extremely high user loyalty, proving that it has quickly become essential for many people in their daily lives.

Another focus going forward will be maintaining the specific attributes that compose the brand personality. Over the past six years, we have had six attributes that we stand for. Yahoo! is fun, friendly, trustworthy, reliable, human, and accessible. As Yahoo! offers more personalization and enters into fee-based services, the trustworthy and reliable components continue to be key, and right now they are clearly what separate us from all the other Internet brands. On the global landscape of all consumer brands, there are no other companies that have been started in the past five years that have established "trustworthy" and "reliable" attributes as well as Yahoo! has. We care about these two attributes very much, because they are important to own to be a leader in any service category. For instance, we have to avoid misguided or poor practices that are not sensitive to privacy or people's feelings about appropriate content, or we could run the risk of losing our strength in these attributes and eroding the meaning of the brand.

On the fun and friendly attribute side, while it might appear frivolous on the surface, these are actually important components to safeguard also. They convey creativity, dynamism, customer care, ease of use, simplicity – all things that are difficult but important for service companies and technology companies to demonstrate and own. Sure, the marketing team and our agency like to have fun, but we really have a loftier objective at heart: It is about Yahoo! being loved, not just respected. It is hard to compete with a brand that puts a smile on your face. Plus, wouldn't it be weird if Yahoo! was no longer fun? How can the company name be Yahoo! and not stand for fun?

Some naysayers in 1996 claimed that the name Yahoo! would be a liability. "Sure, I'll use it to surf around and find Web sites for planning my vacation, but is my grandmother going to track her retirement portfolio on it?" The answer was, yes, grandmothers and investment bankers did and do. And small businesses run their storefronts on Yahoo!, and enterprises run their organizations using Corporate Yahoo!. So in the end, "fun and friendly" are important attributes, as long as they're supported with "trustworthy and reliable." It is the combination of the six attributes that has driven the power of the brand.

Going forward, the other two of the six attributes – human and accessible – will receive increased focus. I think you will see us evolve and extend the brand in terms of humanity to see a much stronger focus on constant improvement in customer service. We get pretty high marks on that, but that's an area where we will be adamant in terms of growing and improving constantly. As we increase the number of services that we charge for, that becomes even more important. Accessibility in the past has meant making sure that anyone, regardless of dial-up or access speed, could have a good experience using Yahoo!. We took that further and have worked to make sure that people could access Yahoo! in multiple languages. These will still be important, but going forward, accessibility also will mean from any device and any location. These ideas of humanity and accessibility are important for companies that want to be leaders in service businesses.

Lastly, in terms of evolving – as to where do we go from here – I think you will see us emphasize more our "evolution and creation." This is about positioning Yahoo! as leading from a technology and innovation standpoint. Does this sound as though it contradicts my belief against a focus on technology? It does and it doesn't. Basically, we need to be innovative to maintain our leadership status. We think that now is the time when we've cultivated an important, opinion-leading audience, which we want to remain loyal to us. While ease of use, simplicity, and friendliness were the hooks that got them in originally, we want to make sure that they continue to be satisfied and feel that they are not being left behind.

The good news is that they aren't. The more sophisticated a user is, the more loyal he or she is to Yahoo!. These users recognize the real value of how integrated Yahoo! is. They truly take advantage of all the customization and personalization Yahoo! offers. About four years ago, there were some competitive services that touted their superior search technology. I was often asked if people who were used to Yahoo!, which is fun and easy, would eventually graduate to these other search services. I confidently said no because our data shows that the savviest users value our integrated approach, which cuts across a variety of services, such as mail, shopping, news, and finance. There have also been questions about whether users will migrate from Yahoo! to niche or vertical services. Again, our integrated approach is a great advantage over this: Very few people are one-dimensional. For instance, an avid sports fan also needs to plan his vacation, pay his bills, and do last-minute holiday shopping online. He might also meet a woman interested in, say, bossa nova, which he knows nothing about, and want to learn as much about it as he can. You never really know what you'll need to know, which is why Yahoo! is essential to people – it continues to be relevant in all aspects of your life. So the bottom line is: I think you will see us introduce a broader range of advanced offerings to the people who are ready for it. And you will start seeing us lead that broader mass audience into a more deep, personalized, and customized relationship.

Favorite Marketing Tools

I am a big believer in advertising of all sorts. To me it's about making sure you use the right media for the right message. Television has been great for some of the things we have wanted to communicate, and that's why we were the first Internet company to advertise on TV. We set the bar high, and although we could barely afford to do it, we knew if that was the case for us, then none of our direct competitors probably could afford it, either.

We looked at other marketing tools, as well. We did a lot of live events. I personally spent time with reporters helping them get online. We were evangelists not just for Yahoo!, but also for the Internet in general. For most people, their first interest in the Internet and Yahoo! was through word of mouth. To stimulate this, we wanted to get as many people as possible to have their first encounter with the Internet through Yahoo!, through a direct personal contact. I will never forget one of the events I attended – it was a microbrewery festival sponsored by public television in the Bay area. In 1995, these were definitely upscale, educated, urban types of folks. We had a few Yahoos demonstrating how to use the Internet and Yahoo!. We literally had people say, "Look honey, there's the Internet!" It was really compelling. Was that a strategic implementation that could scale? No. We weren't in every hometown, but we were in strategically smart places. We were the first to be there, and we had tremendous passion and commitment. We had employees volunteering to do this. The marketing team was out all the time. It was important learning; there is nothing like hearing the consumer directly.

Along those lines of thinking, in 1996, we launched a series of local sites. We were in people's neighborhoods in

Dallas, Fort Worth, Washington, Minneapolis, and Boston at a time when there were no Internet companies in those areas. That was something that also worked in our favor. In a sense, these were the important steps in taking ownership of the category.

Going Forward: the Future of Marketing

I believe that the Internet will play a much more significant role in the future of marketing. Right now, we are working on using our own network to promote our services to our users. Our goal is to try to put the right service in front of the right person. We did a program recently with a series of very high and world-famous designers like Michael Graves and Paul Frank. The goal here was to have very influential designers design ads on Yahoo! to really showcase the medium and to show how cool ads can be in this environment. It gave us some really great ideas, and we hope it has inspired our clients to look at ways to do advertising on the Internet that will be a lot more dynamic than what has happened in the past. You will see more of that.

When I speak publicly, I will often show old television commercials from the 1950s. They were horrible, promotional; they had low production value and were not creative or engaging. It helps to illustrate the point that in the early days of a medium, as was the case with television and now the Internet, it takes a lot of creativity to fully exploit commercial potential. We are just at the beginning with Internet advertising. We have done some things with Pepsi, Britney Spears, Ford, the movie *Pearl Harbor.* What came out of these programs was a new and innovative way to look at the creative possibilities of online and integrated programs, and I believe this is the future of marketing.

Any company that would advertise on the Super Bowl or Major League Baseball should look at these types of programs and should consider taking advantage of this and work with us to help meet their objectives. If you are into brand building and can justify spending that kind of money for thirty seconds, and are ignoring the Internet, then you are missing a huge opportunity. Obviously I am biased, but I think everything points to the fact that the Internet is going to become more and more significant, as opposed to less. The technology is improving, and it is only going to get better. The Internet will only become more and more essential to your life. The more you put into it, the more you get out of it. The challenge as a marketer is people who are going to personalize their information and invest their time with only one major resource.

Another enormously powerful area in the future of marketing is wireless Internet applications. Wireless access has the promise of being the ultimate intervention vehicle. I say that in a positive way – the ability to intervene in a user's activities wherever and whenever could be very convenient for the user and advantageous to us.

Privacy and Policy Issues

With our goal of maintaining strong, loyal, personal relationships with people, it's critical that we have the highest standard of privacy policies. We err on the side of being as sensitive as possible to our users and partners. It's about trust, reliability, and making sure that we do get enough information, so we can give people the experience that we believe will be in their best interest. The more information that a user gives us, the more we are able to present the services, discounts, and offers that a user might want, as well as to establish the best possible policies to reinforce that relationship.

Managing During Turbulent Markets

The biggest challenge in a turbulent time is to really stay focused on the long term. It's hard when you are a new and nimble company. We've grown very quickly. We have people who work here who are built for speed. But in some cases, and I believe in a positive way, things have settled down. We are also in the position where we can reevaluate our strategies. We have brought in some senior management who are really committed to evaluating, strategizing, and building our strong core assets for the long term.

There is a lot of data that supports a consistent brand strategy for the long term. If you look at any economic downturn in the past, the companies that continue to invest in brand building during those times have clearly reaped the rewards. It's a deadly step to cut marketing and brand development during economic downturns because it is a very difficult thing to try to rebuild later, and a downturn is a prime opportunity to steal share from the weak competitors. We are trying to keep as high a profile as we can, and keep the brand in front of people as a sign of assurance, confidence, and leadership.

What it Takes to Become a Leader

I believe that the most important thing as a leader is to have something that you are strongly committed to and stand for. When people are clear about what you stand for, then you make it easier for them to have faith in you and follow you. There will be some people who won't follow you, and that will be clear from the start.

At the beginning, when I first started working at Yahoo!, I basically had to pitch myself. They weren't looking for someone like me; there was no job opening for head of brand marketing. I approached the executive team and told them they needed someone who does what I do. What I stood for was brand building. I was committed to turning Yahoo! into a household name. Many people I would tell this to would laugh. I told any person I hired – the ad agency I worked at, the PR firms and the research companies – that making Yahoo! a household name and global was my commitment. To jump start this, I hired Black Rocket within my first two months, and we brainstormed and researched our target. We talked to consumers. I read every piece of consumer mail the first couple of months to get a sense of why people liked the brand and what some issues were. We conducted some quantitative analysis. After that I summarized what the brand stands for, and the six attributes that we would measure and the standards we would achieve in terms of awareness and market share. I was very clear about our objectives and my commitment.

Continuity is also very important to me. When leaders switch their mission every three months, it makes it pretty hard for anyone to follow. While I strive for creativity, new ideas and innovation, I try to resist the temptation to make changes that disrupt continuity. That is often a tough balance to strike.

The hardest part of being a leader is knowing when to really stand for your commitment and when, for political or other reasons, you need to compromise. I struggle with that. I am not always the most popular person. Sometimes I am accused of being politically naïve; it would be a lot easier at times to cave to pressure and give attention to a broader range of our business areas than to focus heavily on our brand and a small handful of top priorities.

For selling my vision at Yahoo! for new initiatives, I point to our brand track record. It is about constant measurement and evaluation. For what appears to be a fun, friendly, irreverent brand, we spend a lot of time and effort seriously evaluating our research. I work with a lot of people who have consumer and international and local-geography backgrounds who do this. We are constantly measuring and evaluating, and I think that allows us to make a strong case to the executive team when selling something new. We have to take risks in terms of marketing strategies, but at the end of the day, it comes down to the people in the company trusting us, based on our evaluations and prior performance.

Getting Noticed and Keeping Your Edge

I think that it is easy to get noticed; just get the results. Once Yahoo! became a big brand, some people who found this fascinating and wanted to know who was behind it, "marketing our marketing" was never part of my agenda. I'm flattered that many business people admire our marketing, but I care more about whether they like the brand, use the service, and want to advertise on it.

I struggle with staying on top of all of the rapid changes in our industry and broader economic and cultural factors that shape consumer behavior worldwide. No matter how much time I devote to this, I always feel it should be more. I have worked in marketing for 15 years, and one of the ways to make great work happen is to be open to ideas from everywhere and everyone. We have a great team with diverse interests and skills. We need people who have broad areas of expertise and love to share ideas. When I have a team meeting that is supposed to be 45 minutes, sometimes it ends up running two hours over. What happens is a constant sharing of ideas, thoughts, and observations. It's creating an open forum for people to be able to share their ideas and be free in expressing themselves, and often what results is some of our best work. I like to get ideas all the time from people throughout the company, not just in marketing.

The Importance of Setting Goals

Setting goals is critical. I tend to be a long-term goal person. This gets back to my management style. I have certain things that I'm committed to – what the brand stands for, our leadership position vis-à-vis our competitors, our team dynamics, etc. – but I trust my team to develop the short-term goals for achieving the necessary things to make this happen.

The Golden Rules of Marketing

Give people both emotional and rational reasons to use your product and service.

Be authentic.

Don't try to spend your way into leadership. Typically, some of the best ideas we have had been when we didn't have a budget.

Stay focused on your own strategy and commitment, and don't be reactive to competitors.

The Future of Marketing

The communications aspect of marketing is definitely going to get harder. Marketers have abused the attention of consumers for too long. When I see bad advertising, it drives me nuts because, with so much "stuff" out there, it is making it harder for the good communication to get noticed. More things – in both work and leisure – compete for people's time. Eventually people are just going to tune out all but essential communication.

In addition, as the marketing world evolves, how and where we target consumers will change. You really have to market in an integrated way where you need to be present in a lot of places simultaneously. Unfortunately, that becomes less cost efficient and more challenging to manage.

While communications will become more difficult, research will become a lot more efficient and effective. The Internet is setting a whole new standard for speed and comprehensiveness in consumer research. This will definitely facilitate the testing and launching of new products and entry into new markets, both demographically and geographically.

Moreover, there can never be enough emphasis on the importance of a global marketing strategy, even if your company doesn't appear to be international at the onset. This is becoming increasingly important, as the world becomes more globally linked. We work globally, and in most countries we have been very successful in going in early and establishing our brand and service. Companies that are starting out need to have an international strategy right away. And larger, more established companies that are introducing new products need to be quick with an international plan; otherwise, local upstarts can utilize the same formula to win before the "global leader" even enters the local market.

Recognized as an award-winning brand builder, Karen Edwards was a key force behind developing Yahoo! Inc. as a leading Internet brand and one of the fastest-growing global brands among consumers. Edwards was at Yahoo! from January 1996 to September 2001 and formed the brand management team responsible for all advertising, research, promotions, corporate communications, and community relations for Yahoo!'s diverse consumer and business audiences worldwide.

Prior to joining Yahoo!, Edwards worked at Twentieth Century Fox Home Entertainment as a director of business operations in France, Spain, and Italy, and as director of marketing for North America. Edwards' earlier experience includes brand management at The Clorox Company, account management at BBDO for Apple Computer, and public affairs at Chevron USA. Edwards received her M.B.A. from Harvard Business School and holds a B.A. in communications from Stanford University. Her recent honors include American Marketing Association Marketer of the Year (1999), Advertising Age Interactive Marketers of the Year (1999), MC Magazine Marketers of the Year (1998), BrandWeek Marketers of the Year (1997), Advertising Age Marketing 100 (1996), and Advertising Age Digital Media Masters (1997).

MAKING SURE THE CONSUMER HAS A SEAT AT THE TABLE

MICHAEL LINTON

Senior VP – Strategic Marketing

Best Buy

The Role of Marketing

There are multiple roles for marketing in any company. I focus on marketing as being the voice of the consumer and the key link between the company and those consumers. Marketing helps drive a business by representing the consumer and coordinating the dual needs for customer satisfaction and company profit. Marketing should complement and coordinate the rest of a company's tools into a competitive consumer benefit that helps the company achieve its profitability objectives. Moreover, the marketing function also is responsible for claiming that benefit in the marketplace through positioning and messaging.

Marketing is not a function that works alone. It must connect to the operating model of the company and help deliver results that matter (usually long-term profitability). To do that, marketing must always understand how other tools in the company impact consumers and are coordinated to deliver the key consumer benefit. When I think of marketing, I think of marketing as ensuring that the consumer always has a seat at the table.

Great marketing requires an understanding of a number of things: the business of the company, the product category, the marketplace, and the position of your brand. One size of marketing does not fit all situations or all companies. The best marketing starts with an honest evaluation and understanding the marketplace and the brand. This leads to an understanding of what marketing tools should be used to drive the company. Different situations and different companies require different tools. In consumer goods, the major levers usually are product news, advertising, sales focus, packaging, and trade money. In insurance, it's more about distribution, pricing, and speed to market in terms of how quickly marketers can apply the information.

Certain categories are not harder or better than others. All categories are simply different from one another and therefore require different tools in different doses. In retail branding, for example, brand advertising, promotional advertising, and the ability to deliver a better consumer operating experience are critical to success. Both the retail store and the Internet site need to change constantly to provide a constant stream of updated products, services, advertising, and pricing. Delivering a brand-building message requires significant coordination and day-to-day flexibility. Retailers also need to account for the health of the business and the marketplace and have a very honest evaluation of the health and position of the brand. While it's great to have a long-term vision, the truth is that a lot of the brands can't grow due to poor positioning and limited funds. If a brand is fortunate enough to start from a position of strength, it usually allows the company to increase the leverage of its marketing tools.

Marketing Plans

A successful marketing plan builds from an objective starting point and should result in more loyal consumers and long-term profit by improving the brand's position versus competition. The balance of long-term and short-term is critical – for example, sacrificing price in the short term to get market share usually won't cut it in the long run. Some dot-coms did exactly that. In the end, they found out that just selling below cost does not build a brand.

At Best Buy, we use a lot of consumer research to direct the evolution of our brand positioning, marketing tools, and consumer operating model. We sell different categories and different vendor brands. We want to understand why consumers shop Best Buy and our competitors, what products they need and combine with other products (PCs, ISPs, printers, and digital cameras, for example), and what they want out of our store and operating model. The tools we use are driven by what that research tells us, where we want to end up two years from now, and our own judgment. One of the reasons Best Buy embraced the "clicks and mortar" model before it was a widespread concept was research. We never believed consumers would think there was a major difference between BestBuy.com and a Best Buy store. That has proven to be true – customers do not find a brand difference. When they go to BestBuy.com, they are at Best Buy, and vice versa. We have been building this concept into our marketing for two years, and research is telling us to continue.

There are a number of key strengths and attributes that Best Buy wants to have recognized as special elements of our brand. Best Buy is a great place to get the latest in technology and a fun place to shop, and it provides good value and great assortment to consumers. This totals up to our benefit of making our customers' time more fun and more productive.

We have more technology and entertainment consumers than anybody in the marketplace because we focus on delivering that benefit to consumers who need it. Best Buy appeals to the consumers who use those new technologies. While they aren't building their own computers, they are embracing new technology, such as broadband, DVD, and wireless. We have a great consumer in the store who understands what we are, and we keep working to deliver the latest and greatest technology to them in a way they want to buy it. We constantly set the promise for them via advertising: Best Buy is a fun place to shop where you can test, try, and find all of the stuff that is important to you.

We deliver that message through various media, each used in a unique way. The Sunday newspaper insert is designed to drive the consumer to the store for a specific promotional offer. TV and magazines set a long-term brand promise and drive loyalty by building the brand attributes discussed earlier. The Internet and direct mail drive specialized CRM (customer relationship management) messaging. Radio builds our reach and delivers specific promotional events very well.

Our branding advertising sets the promise that Best Buy will "turn on the fun." We deliver that promise in a number of ways, including product assortment, no-commission selling, presentation and environment, and encouraging consumers to play with the technology. We respect consumers for coming to the brand and try to create an environment for them to see and feel these products. We also use the Internet to make it convenient, provide information, and increase assortment.

Today's consumer demands and appreciates a retail brand that can help simplify the complicated world of technology. While it's always been important to have a strong brand at retail, I believe it is now more important than ever because of the digital age. Digital products are complicated and expensive, and they inevitably connect with other digital products to act in concert for a benefit (DVD players, digital TVs, speakers, and DVD movies). This drives consumer purchase patterns. Consumers are looking for retailers that deliver digital answers, not just retailers that sell them products.

The days of buying a VCR and having your biggest problem be the setting of the clock are over! Consumers will not visit ten different companies (or sites) and buy an entire home theater system piece by piece, then contract separately for a satellite dish, service, and assembly. Consumers need faith in the manufacturer and the retail brand. Consumers are not buying a PC; they are buying education for their kids, connections to their friends, and games and entertainment. A number of different products and services need to come together to maximize the benefit, and no one manufacturer makes everything they need. We try to objectively understand what consumers want when they arrive, and try to "make their time better" in a number of ways.

Branding

Brands exist because they deliver a benefit that is so unique and distinctive that the consumer seeks them out. Great brands usually are so associated with a consumer benefit that they "own that benefit" singularly. Maintaining that benefit requires constant vigilance and work. There are lots of great brands, and they all own a benefit. For example, Nike probably owns "best shoe for athletic performance." Disney owns "destination for family entertainment," and

ESPN owns "destination for televised sports." A brand is "owned" by the millions of consumers who credit it with its benefit and attributes.

If you forget your benefit, don't constantly improve your benefit, or forget to study the target consumer who is at the cutting edge of that benefit, your brand will get passed by new brands that deliver the benefit better and "steal" your consumers. It takes constant effort to keep from losing your way – never forget that your brand has to deliver a benefit better than anyone else to become and stay great.

So marketing never finishes building a brand because brands can always go to the next level. Once you stop improving, you get passed and beaten. Honesty is required to take a brand to the next level – an honest understanding of what your brand is good at and where it is vulnerable. There are a lot of good brands, but few truly dominant brands – brands with huge top-of-mind awareness and a controlling market share position. Brands grow by knowing their position in the marketplace; analyzing market share, share of wallet, and consumer preference; constantly talking to consumers; watching key performance and attitudinal attributes; and studying competition. These are all measures best used with a huge dose of objectivity. I try to look at a broad range of measures and believe it's key to compare measures and performance against your industry as well as world-class performers in other industries.

I am usually very focused on the target consumers. How do they feel about the brand and the benefit? While we sample the general population, we really drill down with the target. For example, many consumers know about the Internet, but the smaller group that has already purchased from Best Buy has a wealth of learning and information for us. How did they use "clicks and mortar"? What did they buy and use next? What problems did they have? That's how we try to stay ahead of that curve. These learnings help us evolve our marketing, product offerings, media, and operating model accordingly.

The Evolution of Marketing

The Internet is the most visible way marketing has evolved – driven by the ability to get data, analyze that data faster, drive toward 1:1 marketing, and increase the power of every available tool. The Internet can provide nearly instant information. Other information from the operating model is also virtually instant because of digitization (point of sale, for example) and the speed at which it can be analyzed. Companies can now customize pricing and assortments and have flexibility in manufacturing and delivery. I also think media has changed a great deal. If you go back 20 years, there weren't many ways to get information: a few television channels, magazines, newspapers, and radio. Now there are a couple of hundred television channels (you can even get television on your PC), highly advanced direct mail, and highly targeted magazines. The ability to reach the consumer individually with a tailored message has also changed dramatically.

An example of combining new and old tools is using the Internet and the brick and mortar business in a combination consumers find optimal. There are things the Internet does that brick and mortar cannot, and vice versa. The ability to combine those with the consumer in the center is powerful. For example, Best Buy customers may buy products online and return them to the store or pick them up at the store. The Internet can also provide a larger assortment than brick and mortar. However, brick and mortar lets consumers see and hear things that are important in the purchase decision.

Brick and mortar also allows for the immediacy of being able to use the purchase instantly and the enjoyment of the shopping experience. The key is to effectively combine the two to expand the power of the brand.

As discussed earlier, most consumers do not discriminate across channels, and we've made it our goal to take an established brand like Best Buy and show the customer the site in a way that connects with the store. Best Buy has loyalty and recognition, an advantage most dot-com brands do not have. As an aside, I believe creating a new brand is just as difficult in cyberspace as it is in bricks and mortar. Cyberspace brands still need to deliver a unique benefit, find a way to attract the consumer, and deliver the benefit over time. Many Internet companies tried to build an instant brand without delivering a true benefit. Those brands usually made a consumer promise they couldn't keep.

While many new brands recently emerged, few have currently established a unique benefit that threatens established brands. In general, I think launching a new brand is as difficult as ever – some are successful; most fail. I do think that the digital age has created many new tools to help launch a brand and probably shortened the time required to establish the brand.

Marketing Leadership and Management

Solid leadership and strong brand management skills, creativity, relationship skills, and analytics are all required for strong marketing. Leaders must encourage and build both the creative and the math components of marketing and blend them as appropriate for the situation. Often the leader must work to integrate marketing into the company. While Procter & Gamble is a company that is naturally focused on consumers, other companies are not, and marketing competencies must be integrated into the operating model and the daily, monthly, and yearly business rhythms to succeed.

I try to build a solid marketing team with a diverse range of skills. When I look for people, I look for talent, teaming ability, and specific skill sets. For example, pricing is a very distinct skill set. People do not just walk out of school as great pricing leaders. They need strong analytics, IT basics, and solid conceptual skills – in addition to being great at math. Creative product is not something the leader can just demand or invent. I look for creatives who can deliver a large number of ideas, take criticism, evolve ideas over time, and play on a team. The true power of marketing is achieved when the math and the creative are coordinated quickly and naturally.

The thing I like most about marketing is the challenge of coordinating analytics and creativity to deliver a stronger, better-positioned brand. Consumers notice creativity, and the creative product sets the consumer promise. The component not as readily seen is the disciplined use of math. The analytics that tell you how your creative is doing, where your consumers come from, and how your marketing efforts need to be changed. These factors need to be consistently evaluated in an objective way. That's the discipline of the math in combination with the power of the creative.

The two elements are incontrovertibly linked. Brands need to be creative to be noticed, but leaders can't just bet on great creativity forever without some discipline because sooner or later that creativity will miss. Without a math process to signal that miss, the brand will have no idea what is happening, and it's critical to catch mistakes early. If you air a bad campaign or put out a bad product, you can recover – but only if you know. If not, you can damage your brand significantly. Competition can pass you if you're without objective measures.

On the other hand, if you run everything by the math book, never upgrading the creative or trying new programs or tools, you'll end up with a dull and boring brand, and companies that are more creative will inevitably pass you. You have to do both with balance.

I try to stay current about marketing in a number of ways. First, Best Buy is a place where there are many different marketing issues, and I learn a lot from the job. Second, I talk to the consumers and the Retail team. Third, I look outside my industry. I actually like going to the grocery store, for example. Finally, I have a network of people who love to talk marketing, so I hear about a lot. One of the good things about marketing is that everyone, at heart, is a little bit of a marketer and will talk about it, often without prompting! It's rare to mention that you work with advertising or marketing and not have people give you an opinion or two.

Michael Linton, Best Buy's senior vice president, Strategic Marketing, is responsible for creating product lineups and services that meet customers' needs for technology and entertainment now and in the future.

Linton's experience spans more than 20 years. Before joining Best Buy in January 1999, Linton worked for Remington Products Corporation as vice president of Marketing. Prior to that, he served as the vice president and general manager of a product category at James River Corporation.

A native of Ohio, Linton earned his bachelor's degree from Bowling Green State University and his master's from Duke University. He also serves on the Junior Achievement Upper Midwest board of directors.

BUILDING A POWERFUL MARKETING ENGINE

JODY BILNEY

Verizon

Senior Vice President, Brand Management and
Marketing Communications

Area of Expertise

My specific area of expertise is in general management. The definition of marketing that I grew up with is that marketing is general management. Marketing begins with strategy development and includes execution and all points in between. It is using the principles of marketing to achieve financial objectives for an organization. In all of the businesses and industries where I have worked, almost all the products I have marketed were parity products. Marketing is often the challenge of trying to create a preference for products that are very similar and are regulated to be that way. For example, in the case of household cleaning products, Dow Bathroom Cleaner and Lysol Basin, Bath & Tile cleaner are not meaningfully different. The main difference is using the "Scrubbing Bubbles" character to speak of the benefits on behalf of your product. Marketers create differences to create a preference for the product through marketing, with the ultimate goal to drive the financial objective of the brand.

The Challenges of Marketing

As a marketer right now, if you like a challenge, then you are in luck. In very few categories or industries are there sustainably differentiated products. You have to create relevant, compelling differences to earn preference. With the advances in technology, differences between products are so short-lived, and every other product can do what your product can do so quickly, that any difference you have must be capitalized on immediately. You have to link what is new or more advanced with your brand to create that association and own the benefits of what is new because very quickly, from a capabilities perspective, everyone else is going to be able to do what you do as well. As a marketer, that is a huge challenge.

Marketers need to find those angles on their business and with their product so that they can create a connection with customers. You have to connect with customers on a lot of levels. First, you have to connect with them on a practical level. You have to demonstrate that your product or service has a benefit that is relevant to them. Then, you have to connect with them on an emotional level to sustain a relationship, so they like doing business with you. Next, you have to connect with customers on an intellectual level, so they know you are the right company for them to do business with. Achieving all of that in an environment where there is very little difference between products is a huge marketing challenge. That's the fun of it! In residential telecom, customers can't tell the difference between dial tones. Dial tone is dial tone! You have to create a reason to do business with your company when inherently there is no product difference.

Building a Great Brand

From a practical standpoint, to have a great brand, you need a great product or service. The basics have to be in place. You can try forever to be a great brand, but if you don't have a product backing it up, it will never happen. I think some of the brands generated in the recent dot-com hoopla were potentially established, like pets.com. But were they great brands? I would say no, they're not great brands. You need a great product or service. You need the fundamentals in place.

The next part of establishing a great brand is that you have to connect with people on the levels that I mentioned before – practical, emotional, and intellectual. You have to make those connections and perform consistently, so they always have the same great experience with your brand. You want people to choose your brand "just because"; they don't have a decision to make. They choose your brand because it is easy for them to choose it, and there is really no decision for them to make; your brand is their habit! When you've accomplished that, then you have a great brand. When you take the overt decision-making process away from people, they just know they want to do business with you, and sometimes they are not able to articulate exactly why. They just know it's the right choice for them. That's when you've got a consistently great brand. You have to have a great product for that to happen, and you need to have made connections with people on all different levels.

Sustaining a Great Brand

How do you sustain a great brand? The first part of the answer is an easy one. You have to support the brand and have money behind it. As a corporation, you have to have a fundamental belief that your brand is of great value, that it drives sales, and that it drives financial performance. You have to believe that your brand plays a significant role in the success of your organization. If you believe that, you are more likely to consistently spend on your brand, and this is something that has to be done.

Along with that, you have to have some foresight. You have to have foresight and be able to anticipate market, technology, competitive, and social shifts. That's part of being a marketer and being a brand builder. If you like where your industry is going, you have to position yourself in a way to be first. If you don't like where it's going, you have to find a way to affect it so that your brand stays relevant to people in changing times. It seems to me that the brands that have fallen behind are the brands that don't stay contemporary. They might fall behind from a technology or societal perspective. Times change, and attitudes evolve, and unless you stay current with that, your brand will fade. You have to keep your products current and keep communicating their benefits in a compelling way to your customers. Your brand will be kept current with this mindset and organization discipline.

Situations That Can Kill a Brand

Disasters happen and, if mishandled, can kill a brand. For instance, it will be fascinating to see how the whole Firestone situation with the Ford Explorers goes. Today, odds are about 50/50 as to which brand is less damaged and even survives. Another example is years ago when Audi cars sprang into gear by themselves, lurched forward, and pinned people against their garages. At the time that was happening with Audi, they were makers of an upscale foreign car. They were unique and were gaining penetration. I am not sure that this situation was handled very well, or that their brand recovered and had the same position and potential in the marketplace that they might have had before. Not that their brand is dead, but they needed to be more clear on why that happened, how badly they felt about it, and what they did to fix it, so you could trust the Audi brand as a car you want to be driving. There are things that can happen to a brand that, if not handled well, can cause the brand to lose value and relevance. When consumers lose trust, it is very difficult to regain. There are lots of others on the flip side that handled disaster really well and improved their brand's standing. Finally, another way to kill a brand is to stop investing in it.

Honing the Marketing Message

From the big picture's perspective, you attempt to create a point of difference or an angle that your brand can own and stand for. Brand communications establish brand positioning. There are some tried and true quantitative and qualitative research techniques that assist in honing your brand message. There is nothing particularly revolutionary there. Depending on what agency or consultant you have, they will have their own coined process. What we try to do is create an "umbrella position" in the marketplace that is broad enough for all of our products to be marketed underneath and be promoted and sold very aggressively. We have a two-pronged approach: (1) We establish an umbrella brand, and then (2) we give people a reason to buy our product and participate in our promotions on a product-by-product basis.

There are all sorts of ways to stay current with the customer. I am sure you have heard of the Yankelovich Monitor. There are half a dozen of those services that Verizon subscribes to. We look at all of that information, then synthesize it ourselves, given what we know about technology, competitors, etc. We see what makes the most sense and what is most relevant for our categories and geography, so we can address what we need to be concerned about. Then we make product enhancements and make sure our communications stay relevant as things are evolving. There are other specific things we do, as well. For instance, for the youth market, we have a stable of young people who are in different places around the country, and when we are introducing things that we think are relevant to them, we go to this panel. We do that several times a year. We have some kids in Boston, Dallas, and Los Angeles; we have them around the country. This is different from a focus group because we have a regular dialogue with them to help stay current and help anticipate future needs and interests.

Favorite Marketing Tools

There is much discussion about how to spend dollars most effectively. Rarely are you in a no-constraints kind of budget situation. If I were in the no-budget-constraints fantasy world, the best approach would be the marketing plans that are coordinated. I didn't use the word integrated, but coordinated, because there is an important distinction.

The best plan depends on what you are trying to accomplish in the marketplace, of course. In 1996, when I worked at GTE Directories, the yellow pages and phonebook division, one of our jobs was to introduce Super Pages, online yellow pages, and more. At the same time, we were trying to update perceptions on the yellow pages product. It's a 75-year-old product that people don't think twice about. We decided an interesting way to generate interest in those households, introduce Super Pages, and update the Yellow Pages was through kids. Kids are big influences and are quick to adapt to new technology. We realized this might be an interesting angle that hadn't been tried before.

We then created a bus tour. We customized six buses, with cool graphics outside and souped-up technology inside, went to schools, and introduced the Internet and Super Pages by donating computers to each school. At the same time, we also had a promotion with Happy Meals at McDonald's. We inserted mini yellow pages directories in Happy Meal bags. We had a relevant product that was interesting and useful and that fit strategically with McDonald's. We were able to get at kids with the product, and parents could see that, as well. Those two things were not completely integrated – the form wasn't exactly the same – but it was the same strategy "coordinated," using the same angle with kids. That's a way that allows you to be creative, but you don't have to be hooked completely together with everything from a graphics and messaging perspective. Unconstrained coordinated marketing efforts allow you to use all of your creative abilities and can really ignite some dynamite promotions.

Another approach we are using at Verizon is an integrated approach, where each vehicle carries the same message and creative look. Each works and builds on the other. An effort may be supported by DirecTV, direct mail, and a telemarketing component. It may feature the same product, promotion, and scripting but comes at it from different media. People consume media differently, so we come to them with the same message in a different way. This works, too. If you don't have cost constraints, and you can do something that is coordinated and lets you approach things from different angles, that works very well. Or, if you are very single-minded and can do something integrated across multiple forms of media, then that can work, too. They have to be either coordinated or integrated if you have lots or little amounts of money; otherwise, neither will be as effective.

Evaluating Your Advertisement Campaign

We measure a lot and try hard to make sure every dollar is spent as efficiently as it can be. Let me give you some of the measures we use. First, the reason we do any marketing is to generate revenue. The sales we produce are a critical measure. We also track to ensure we are enhancing key brand attributes. We also try to measure our impact on customer relationships via loyalty indicators. We know that if we sell customers more products from our portfolio and meet more of their needs, chances are they will be more loyal to us. The final category is how well the campaign was executed. Did we execute it without hampering the operations of the firm? Was it executed easily in the sales channel? Was it easy for customers to understand? Revenue, brand attributes, customer relationship, efficiency, and execution are all things we rate ourselves on.

The Importance of Innovation

Innovation is always an aspiration. Whatever we do, or communicate, we always hope that this is the thing that will be breakthrough. To be honest, that doesn't happen very often. When it does happen, it is absolutely amazing. You are on a magic carpet for a while. You need to enjoy the ride, because it doesn't happen very much, although each time we try to strive toward that. From a practical standpoint, I can't count on some innovation with each campaign. I can't count on having a breakthrough idea every time we go to market. You have to plan for something that is less than that, but then hope that you are giving the right direction and that your agency is giving the best shot so that there is a breakthrough. If you get something innovative, then your job is that much easier for that short period of time. If you don't, you have to keep plugging away at the basics until your next shot and hope for that innovation the next time.

Part of it is the direction you give your agency partners. It is helpful if you tell them that you absolutely need a big idea here. You can't say that every time, though. It isn't fair or reasonable to say that everything you do all year is of equal importance, so you do need to make sure that you are giving the right direction to your agency. If they know that this is the biggest idea for the year, and this is what they need to focus on, then you will have a better shot at that marketing innovation.

Exciting Effects of Internet and Technology

It's a little confusing right now, exactly how the Internet is going to deliver from a marketing standpoint. What the Internet offers is tremendous transaction efficiency. It is cheaper to take and fulfill an order on the Internet than it is to have a human being answer the phone and do that. We know that the Internet offers us, from a cost side, some tremendous efficiency.

What it offers from the customer's point of view is that they can interact with us at any time. It is on their terms. Whenever they want to, they can do business with us. For some customers, there is a real value in that. For Verizon, we operate domestically from Hawaii to Maine, so we have time zone differences, product differences that can be complicated from a customer service perspective that the

Internet helps us with a lot. From a sales and service perspective, there are some real benefits, expense for the company, and flexibility for the customer.

The Internet is a great place for customers to spend some time gathering information to truly understand more about your products and services. With some of the new telecom products, and in many other categories, as well, things are confusing. Customers can spend some time, research, and look into things. They can make a purchase that they have a great deal of confidence in. A more confident purchase means fewer products are returned because customers have made an informed decision. There are huge marketing effects related to the retention and returns that can happen when customers spend a little time investigating their purchases.

In terms of using the Internet as a communications medium, we haven't had the same sort of success that we've had with more traditional media vehicles, such as direct mail and telemarketing, with response rates and close rates. We are getting better and figuring out how to be effective on the Internet. A few years ago, everyone used banner ads. They were cheap, fortunately, but you got what you paid for in a lot of those cases! Much Internet advertising just has not proved to be as effective as some of the more traditional media. It is still an integral part of any marketing plan. You can't not have it. It needs to be either coordinated or integrated into what your marketing efforts are. But in itself, for our category, it has had less specific impact as a communications vehicle to sell a particular product. Part of that is that it is still new, and we need to get better at using it. We are working on that all the time.

Ideal Marketing Tools

If we could create an ideal marketing tool, with whatever killer app this translates into, we would have something! Right now, we have an interesting dichotomy that exists with customers. On one hand, they tell us they want customized solutions. They only want to know what they want to know, and only want to buy things exactly specific for them. At the same time, they have an enormous concern for privacy. If you think about it from a manufacturer's perspective, you need customer information in order to customize; yet at the same time, customers are concerned for their privacy. The most efficient marketing could occur if customers were comfortable enough to tell us specifically what it is they want and are interested in. Then we would really have something! Right now, when we over-customize, it can be offensive to customers because they think we are dipping into their privacy. From an efficiency perspective, because we are never in those no-budget-restraint times, if we could figure out a way to customize without having people feel as though we've invaded, then we would really have something very efficient and powerful from a marketing perspective.

Applications on the Horizon

People have experience with PCs at their office. Taking the speed and convenience that they experience at their office with broadband to their home is very exciting. Currently, that's what broadband allows a residential customer to do. Broadband is going to evolve even further into entertainment and more. It will be fast, varied, and convenient. I have twin girls who are eleven, and they have homework every night. Having the Internet for them in our house is important. If it is slow, they are so frustrated. Young people expect the highest performance from their PCs, communications, and Internet services.

Young people who have grown up with broadband and people who work in offices expect this in their homes, as well. Wireless has unlimited potential with the busy lifestyles that people have. There isn't any suggestion that life is going to slow down. Consumers are going to continue to be stressed with how busy they are. They are not giving any indication that they are going to slow down. Giving them tools to help them deal with all the things that are going on in their lives is going to be helpful. Wireless does that extremely well. Broadband does also.

Admirable Aspects of Other Marketers

People who stick to their brand purpose and mission are admirable. If you are a publicly traded company, and quarterly earnings are tracked, it is an easy thing for leaders to get distracted and focus only on the short term. Companies that are best at managing their brands seem to have the right appreciation; they value the role of the brand so that they don't consistently cut from their brand-building budgets. When times get tough, they invest in their brand to help stimulate the marketplace. The marketing leaders I respect the most are those who in tough times can maintain their focus on the brand and can continue to build it.

Becoming a Leader

The most effective marketing leaders I have seen are those who have a vision. They have an end game where they want the business to be. They can communicate, inspire, and galvanize their team to want to make it happen. A leader must create a goal or vision that turns on and inspires the work force. It makes so much sense to employees that they want to work in that leader's organization. Those marketers who can create a meaningful end game and then translate that into something the team takes into the marketplace will attract the organization's best people to come work in their group, so they can do exciting work and be a part of something successful. The best employees want to do great work and win. Great marketing leaders attract the best employees.

Let me give you a quick example. When we did that McDonald's promotion, our sales people who walk door-to-door selling yellow pages were able to say we're doing a promotion with McDonald's. It made them feel they were part of something successful before it even happened. If you can make your people feel they are working on something that matters internally or externally, then you are going to get the kind of following that is needed to be effective in an organization. For leadership overall to get the best output from the best employees, leaders must be sure employees understand and are inspired by the direction they are leading them in.

Skills on a Marketing Team

The kinds of skills you need on a marketing team are creative, tenacious, accountable, resilient, and flexible. In some cases it is important that the team members are experienced, but not in all cases. I would take someone with the above characteristics in a heartbeat over someone who had put out ten programs in the marketplace. If someone is disappointed easily when someone makes a comment, and they get deflated, they are not going to be able to make the impact we need. No marketing group can get anything done by themselves alone. They have to get help from the sales channel, production, or the regulatory area, etc. What a marketer must do is that in each of their interactions, they have to make enough sense that they win a disproportionate amount of mindset from the organization. I want people all around the company to think about my business more than they think about anything else during the day. They won't do that unless they are clear on the goals, what needs to get done, why they are working so hard, and why this is going to be successful. People want to work where they are likely to be successful and where they are having fun.

Staying on Top of Marketing Knowledge

That's a concern. My team and I have talked about this a few times. How do you stay current? It's a big deal. You have to recognize that you can fall behind. If you first recognize that, then you tend to pay a little more attention and seek out new information to make sure that you always challenge yourself. What's the latest? What haven't we done? What don't I know? What have we not been exposed to? You have to make a concerted effort to go find it.

In Verizon, at different times of the year our focus is on different things. The most important time of the year for us is when the year begins. You can imagine that with a recurring revenue stream, when a customer spends a dollar with us in January it's worth twelve dollars for the year. If someone buys something in September, that's only worth four dollars. What that means for us is that we spend a lot of time and energy making sure the first six months are strong. There is another part of the year where we plan, investigate, and look into things. For part of the year, we are all about execution, and in the other part, we focus on making sure we are looking externally inside and outside of our industry, making sure we are current with everything that is going on. It is so hectic, running the business every day, that you have to plan it into your schedule to make sure you are working to say contemporary. Otherwise, you are so caught up in doing what you do every day, soon your skills are dated.

Setting Goals

It is really important to find a balance. Finding the right people who can toggle between creating new ideas, solutions, promotions, etc., but can also get inside the numbers to make sure we are being as efficient as we can, are the most valuable people we can have. How I try to influence this is to make sure I am asking the right questions. If the only questions I ever ask are about the results, my team is only going to analyze. If we bounce on to the next event and never analyze results, we'll never spend as smart as we should. I have to make sure I am asking the right series and sequence of questions at the right time to make sure my organization is thinking about different things at different times.

Today, for example, we are planning for second quarter next year. With this timing, we can create. Not for a whole lot longer, because we have get down to execution, but for now we have been able to create, think, look around, and try to anticipate what is going to make a difference for the firm in the second quarter next year. That's how I make sure my group is looking as comprehensively as they can. We have a group of people who are able to move between these two things effectively in key leadership jobs within the marketing organization.

Finding the Right People for the Marketing Team

I like differences. I like people who have different backgrounds. I like to put them together and have them solve together, knowing their backgrounds will force unique perspectives to be brought forward. It works better some times than others. There are some times when people are so different they can't get on the same wavelength. There are other times – and in my experience, this happens more often than not – the most effective marketing organization is one that has a mix of talent and experience from different industries. With that, they have to have the personal style of being open and collaborative, not judgmental. You can't get a more powerful team than people who have whole different sets of experiences and start creating together.

When we have been trying to do things that were newer and different, we have had marketers from the airline industry, combined with consumer packaged goods people and telecommunication veterans. Getting the breadth of ideas derived from these different experiences creates a very powerful marketing engine. The downside is this combination can sometimes be slower because of the basics to be covered with everybody. Once you get past that, and everybody is not new anymore but can still draw from their background, then you can get some very high-impact solutions. You get very familiar work and output if you have everyone who is only from one industry, say packaged goods or telecom.

The way to get a breakthrough is by mixing it up and getting people who have different perspectives. You need basic differences, not just industry stuff – different ages and experiences. From a Verizon perspective, it has been great. When we merged, the Bell Atlantic part of our company had people who had experience in the Northeast. They were very different from the experience of those people who had been marketing in Texas or California. You can imagine the interesting discussions and the creativity that we have been able to take advantage of when we bring the two together! That's how I like to create it – to get some differences. You have to be careful to get the right blend because you can slow yourself down. You need the right blend of experiences to make a really productive team.

The Future of Marketing

There are some fundamentals I think will always be there for marketers. Marketers absolutely have to stay in touch with the marketplace, with customers, as well as their competitors. There is no way to do productive marketing without that. You have to pay attention to where customers' heads, habits, and attitudes are and how they are evolving. You can't be an effective marketer if you don't understand who your current and emerging competitors are. This is all about business results at the end of day. I can't see that part ever changing.

Interwoven in both the competitors and customers is the role of the brand. As the world gets faster-paced, and as technology changes, there will be some confusion. The role of the brand becomes more important because it will be the one thing that people understand. They understand they can trust Verizon, and they will get the latest technology at a good value. Interwoven within the customer and the competition, the role of the brand is always going to be there. It is going to play an increasingly important role as our lives get even busier, and technology is changing and evolving. These are the ways marketing is going to stay the same. It will have that constant definition, as long as companies are trying to sell stuff. That's what marketing is going to be all about.

It will probably change in some ways too, because there will be new tools and technology. The Internet is going to continue to evolve. Companies are going to get better at using the Internet for marketing purposes. Someone will figure out that killer app that I suggested before – the combination of privacy and customization. The Internet might be the key to that. There have to be changes, and there will be.

Jody Bilney is senior vice president, Brand Management and Marketing Communications for Verizon, responsible for leading corporate-wide initiatives to build and strengthen the Verizon brand worldwide. She also manages centralized advertising, media buying/planning, and direct mail/direct response for the Telecommunications organization.

Prior to her current position, Bilney was president, Consumer Markets for Verizon's Retail Markets Group, responsible for marketing, sales, product management, channel and business development, and strategic planning for consumer markets.

Before the Bell Atlantic/GTE merger, Bilney was vice president, Consumer Markets for GTE Network Services, a position she held beginning December 1998. She was responsible for revenue generation, customer satisfaction, and product performance for all consumer segments serviced by Network Services. Reporting to her were the Product Management, Marketing, National Center Operations, National Credit Management, Phone Marts, and the Customer Contact Centers.

Bilney joined GTE in late 1994 as director, Consumer Market Strategy. She also has served as vice president, Marketing for GTE Directories and as vice president and general manager of Consumer Sales for GTE Communications Corp.

Before joining GTE, Bilney worked at DowBrands, makers of consumer packaged goods, for ten years. There she held a variety of marketing management positions, as well as a position as director, Global New Ventures.

Bilney earned a bachelor's degree in economics with a minor in marketing from Clemson University in South Carolina.

HOW BRANDS AND MARKETING ARE EVOLVING TOGETHER

JOHN HAYES

American Express

Executive Vice President, Advertising & Global
Brand Management

How Marketing is Evolving

I believe in the human element. The mission we established in my group at American Express is accountability for building marketplace demand. I think one of the most rewarding parts of any marketing or branding endeavor is having a product or brand take off and watching its success. It's like having a hit TV show or song. Anything that you can actually watch the public take an interest in, and create a relationship with, is what makes marketing exciting.

I have seen a lot of things change, but at the same time I have seen a number of things stay the same. First of all, there are many new trends happening in the marketing realm, due mostly to the fact that today, more than ever before, we are able to have a dialogue with the consumer. Two-way channels are open and will continue to expand, so that on a real-time basis, we are able to understand what customers need, want, like, and don't like. Having that ongoing dialogue helps perfect marketing and improves the value of a brand.

A brand, as we define it, is really nothing more than the relationship between a product or a company and its customer. That relationship is much more well rounded when we have the channels, as we do today, that allow a dialogue with consumers. That change is profound. Dialogue used to happen on a sporadic and episodic basis with a small group of people. It was never a mass notion. Now, because we're able to converse on the Internet, get feedback, and receive data for analysis, it's becoming one. That's a real change from a marketing standpoint. Closing the loop has been critical and has always been a part of marketing, but it's never been as big or as important as it is today.

The second thing I would say is that marketers and companies are beginning to understand that you build a brand through careful management of a customer experience. There was a time when many people thought that brands were built through advertising. Or that one great ad campaign built a brand. It's just not that way today. There are some brands being built without any advertising.

The way to have an impact on the customer is to take a 360-degree approach to the relationship. You need to surround customers with an experience that will make an impact and get them to feel a certain way about doing business with a company, sometimes even before they become a customer.

Marketing is more sophisticated today because to "surround" a customer, you really need to understand their life – what they want, what they like, and what they don't. It requires using all of the channels that are available in a way that is diverse, but consistent, in terms of messaging through those channels. Marketing is very complex and challenging, but I think new opportunities have evolved that heighten its impact more than ever before.

Exciting Tools

The channels that are open and available to marketers are very exciting. By the way, I don't think the new channels will replace the old ones. They will simply augment the ability to communicate. I think the telephone is still a great medium, as are movie theaters. I think broadband and wireless are exciting because they add a dimension of interactivity. You can make an offer to somebody and then hear back immediately if that offer resonates with the customer.

The segmentation that is being done today is very interesting. The way to build and nurture mass product brands is to rely more and more on your ability to effectively segment the population. To whom are you speaking? What do they need? How does that differ from other customers? How can you reach that customer more effectively by defining them within a segment? Segment marketing is exciting because it provides value on an almost one-to-one basis. I think it will be a long time until we market completely one-to-one, but I think we are better able to examine smaller groups of customers and their collective characteristics.

Building a Brand

In some ways, it's easier to build a brand today because we have more tools than ever before, and a better real-time dialogue. Yet in other ways it's harder, because it's very difficult to create a smoke screen. You aren't going to fool many people for a long period of time. The way to build a brand is by delivering a real experience, by providing real value, and by delivering on the promises you make. If you don't, you'll hear back from customers when they're disappointed or unhappy, and that word of mouth carries very quickly. Today, our world is networked. It's more difficult because not only do you have to come up with a clever promise, but you also have to deliver on that promise consistently, from customer to customer. That's where it gets challenging. Many industries are struggling to deliver on the customer experience, not just coming up with clever positioning lines.

Bringing a brand forward and continuing its reinvention requires a number of things. First, it requires a very clear understanding of how customers define your brand today. It's not beneficial if only people who work for American Express theorize about how to define the brand, because we are not judging it. Really understanding the customer base – how they view your brand today versus how they viewed it yesterday – is very important. The next thing is measuring product delivery against perceived value.

We know some of the key attributes of the American Express brand: trust and the promise to pay. Those are critical attributes of the brand that have been aligned since the 1800s, when one of our lead products was the Travelers Cheque. Those defining elements of the brand are still alive today. Customer service – the kinds of service people expect when you say American Express – is part of this brand, and our customers will tell you that. Many people feel a sense of belonging because it says something about a person when they use the American Express card. Their association with the card can be articulated in a variety of ways, including customers talking about their "member since" date. It's amazing how many of our customers can tell you when they got their first American Express Card – where they lived, how old they were, and what stage of life they were in at the time. I wonder how many products have the same level of attachment.

All attributes of the brand need to be understood. There needs to be a focus within the company, demonstrating that those things are important, and that what the consumer holds to be valuable is important to us. The next step is translating that feeling into new products, offerings, and customer value, predicated on understanding the trends in the market. What are the new demands for payment, for example? Understanding those trends is important. Equally important are the valuable attributes of the brand and how they complement new products in the marketplace. Once you understand the product needs, the psychological needs of consumers, and the history of a customer's relationship with the brand, you have to put it all together.

Ultimately, that's what we did with Blue from American Express. With Blue, we had to understand how to bring a smart card into the marketplace. We had to identify the attributes of American Express that were important within that product. And we had to marry that information with an understanding of the consumer. When we prepared for the Blue launch in April 1999, we found our target audience naturally fell into one of two groups. One group, as they talked about the future, said that the Internet and wireless were amazing and that they loved communicating with people. The other group was contemplating the purchase of a generator with the upcoming Y2K. They thought about how much cash they needed on hand during the year-end, and they were nervous about flying anywhere during the holiday. It was a very interesting bipolarization. Having the millennium as our benchmark helped create an even clearer vision of that polarity.

What was interesting is that we were able to identify a group of people who were optimistic about the future, and who wanted a brand that would embrace the future with them. They said they wanted a brand that would think about new ways to serve them better – not just for the sake of being innovative – and a brand that would be sensitive to where the future is going. We took the American Express brand with its trust, attributes and customer service, and built a brand that understood that these people are optimistic about their future and want us to be part of it. We were able to appeal to a new customer segment by crafting that position for Blue.

Killing an Established Brand

A brand does not have an inalienable right. It takes work, nurturing, and a very clear understanding of the consumer. Product failure, slowness in response to product failure, and not completely understanding what the consumer thinks about your brand can kill it.

Many brands have dealt with product failure; some have survived and some haven't. Why? Those who survived quickly recognized product failure, understood what the customer was thinking, and corrected it. That's how you build a brand and keep it alive.

There are three things that can kill an established brand: (1) complacency, (2) assuming a right to exist in the market, and (3) arrogance. A number of companies have gone through bouts of arrogance, thinking they are unassailable, and basically losing touch with the customer base. They no longer know who their customers are, what they need, whether they are getting the right services, and if they have the right balance between cost savings and customer service. Those variables have to be challenged all the time for the brand to remain healthy.

Keeping in Touch With Customers

I think it's a competitive advantage, and I think it's incredibly important to keep in touch with customers. How do you craft the right message? Ultimately there is inspiration. But you craft the right message by knowing how people responded to the last ten messages you put in the market place – what they thought was interesting and compelling, and what they didn't. I am not a big believer in clinical research. I hate putting communications through clinical steps and focus groups. While we do some of that, I don't like to rely solely upon it. The better your feedback loop is with the real customer in the marketplace, the better you can react to what is really going on. Then you can refine your communications message, be it direct mail, television commercials, or the Internet. The more real-time and the faster you can get the feedback from the customer, the faster you can re-craft the message.

What I love about the new channels of wireless and Internet is that not only does it give you quick feedback from the consumer, but it also allows you to reproduce what you need in a matter of hours instead of weeks, months, or years. Changing and shortening feedback time and response time is exciting because it's an advantage. Consumers know when you've listened. They appreciate being asked what they think. And they appreciate when you respond, demonstrating their mindset in the marketplace. If a marketer can shorten that feedback loop and the response time, it's an enormous advantage.

The Importance of Innovation

Innovation is important. You can't stay in one place. Let's face it, all of us read newspapers in the morning to find out what's new in the world. If you have news, consumers pay attention. They read. They listen. And they think about you because you're offering something new. Innovation in marketing is absolutely critical. You have to keep innovating; otherwise, you lose to the competition. Our marketing experience as a company has involved constant innovation. It is very important.

If you want to be seen and known, innovation helps establish you on the landscape. But innovation alone won't keep you there; it plays only a partial role. The customer experience throughout is critical. There are many things that play a role in the customer experience. If you want to be noticed, innovation certainly helps a product, company, or brand. Innovation can take the form of the channel by which it is communicated. It can offer the customer interaction. Or it can relay a message in a unique way. Innovation needs to be part of the overall marketing mix to be competitive.

Judging a Successful Marketing Campaign

In the simplest sense, I judge a campaign on whether the demand for our product is increasing and if people feel better about our brand. That's the simplest way to determine success. Not every channel is easy to measure. It's an overstatement to say that you can run an ad and be able to know tomorrow, or the week after, whether or not you have been successful. You just don't know until you see the culmination of an overall marketing effort.

If I go back to what was done with the launch of Blue, there were a number of marketing components. We utilized everything from a live event broadcast across the country from Central Park to advertising, and from direct mail to Internet channels. We set goals based on our historical performance, and, from day one, measured the demand we received. Did the phone ring? Did people ask for the product? Did people qualify for the product?

The first measure is whether or not people are attracted to the product. That tells you that the marketing is out there, and that people are aware of it.

Second measure: Are we are getting the right quality of customer? Are we getting customers who can be approved? Once I get those customers, are they using the product? In our case, they buy the product once and keep using it. Having repeated usage and getting people involved are the things we look for. People did not only apply for the card, they identified with it and embraced it. We measured it over time through a variety of key variables: Have they heard about it? Are we getting the right people? Are they using it repeatedly?

Selecting the Right Channels

When we plan an overall launch, we might use eight major marketing channels. With the television channel, I would look for awareness and a level of interest. I am not going to close the sale on television or get somebody to accept an offer because I probably want to customize the offer in a more segmented medium. So the role of that channel would be to create some level of brand awareness or interest.

In the Internet channel, I might want to deliver something that would close the deal, taking, as a starting point, the sense of awareness that has already been created. On this channel the role will be to relay the specifics for the product and why it is necessary. Objectives are divided by different channels. When we enter any marketing effort, we think about it from the standpoint of communicating a product's value and its relationship to the brand, targeting the right channels to reach the right audience, and giving a message from start to finish that will deliver a sale. Obviously this won't happen on every channel. Some channels will open it, while others will close it.

Developing a Marketing Plan

There are some simple steps that we follow that give discipline to the process. The first step is to determine the goal of the project. What are we trying to do – get a million card members, or get people to use the card more? We start off with a very clear articulation of the business goal. To create an effective marketing program, you have to know what you are driving toward. Sometimes it sounds simpler than it is. Sometimes at the beginning of the project the goal has to be clarified.

The second step is defining the target, which we do in two ways: Demographically, by asking the following questions: Who are they? Where do they live? And, secondly, by emotional definition, which is personified by the example I gave you about Blue. Groups of people were optimistic about the future and eager to embrace technology in their lives. When those two steps are completed, we know what we are trying to do from a business standpoint and whom we are trying to reach.

The third step in our approach is positioning. What is the product we are working with, and how do we position it to make it appealing to the target audience?

The fourth step involves deciding which channels to use for communication. If you notice, I haven't talked about the creative product or strategy yet. Channel selection depends upon our audience. If we are talking to tech-savvy people, then tech channels will be more useful than they would be to another group. The target audience helps us select the channels for communication. If they are music-savvy, we may use musical events. If they are small-business people using a PC as their connection to the world, we may find that email is the best way to reach them. So we reflect on the target audience and make our channel selection.

Next, we reflect on our goal. If our goal is to reach out to a new group of people and obtain a large number of new card members in a short period, we know we have to go fairly broad on target audience. We also know that our channels have to reflect that approach. We have to create awareness that we have a product for these people, and then we have to take that awareness down to action. Channels are defined by the goal we have established and the target audience. Once we have nailed down the channel, we move to the presentation of the product to the customer, through the channels. Instead of creating a television commercial, we begin by knowing the channels we want to use and create communication that works within them: live events, Internet, direct mail, television, and outdoor posters. The channels have to be nailed down first.

The last steps are creative strategy and ongoing communications. Frequently companies will do a major launch and will not pay attention to ongoing communications and how they continue to nurture a customer base. Finally, we define and measure success. If

I have a clear goal, then metrics help me know how I'm doing against it. From the beginning, the measurement of success helps people focus and relates back to the goal. The last piece is brand health. What impact is this going to have on the brand health, and what are the measures? We go into the marketplace and measure the key-initiatives impact the project has had on the brand's health.

Admirable Aspects of Other Marketers

The people who impress me the most are those who have been innovative: Those who have not only identified the obvious new channels, but who have used channels effectively to create experiences for customers. I am impressed by those marketers who create a customer experience and manage it carefully. That's a difficult thing to do. It requires many people and a large organization. To get everyone to execute consistently, and to give customers a consistent experience, is very challenging. I am in awe of organizations and the people who accomplish that.

Becoming a Leader in Marketing

First of all, I think individuals who succeed in marketing need to like people and have to be interested in what drives their behavior. Marketing touches the human element every day. You have to enjoy people, and you have to enjoy human nature, or you won't be good at it. You also have to be resilient. As in any industry, what's the ratio of failures against success? New films with great actors aren't always successful. You have to be resilient because not everything is going to work.

Third, I would say you have to have thick skin, because everything you do is public. There is nothing private about your work. Everyone in the company knows what has worked well and what hasn't. You can't become discouraged by the people who vocally state that they don't like something, because it might work in the marketplace.

You have to be willing to take risks in a way that creates news and customer demand.

Staying on Top

Staying on top of knowledge starts with reading publications that help reflect where people are today. That's why I like *USA Today*; it's about culture, society and the marketplace. I may skim *The Wall Street Journal* and *The New York Times* because being up to speed on business is also important, but *USA Today, People, Time* and *Newsweek* are key, as are magazines like *Fortune* and *Forbes.* I enjoy those "conventional wisdom" boxes and polls; I find that data from these publications helps me understand consumer viewpoints.

I surf the Internet and watch television. In regard to television, it's important for me to be in touch with different age groups. Sometimes I watch "Road Rules" on MTV, or some of the "Behind the Music" on VH-1, or E biographies. If you meet somebody interested in baseball, they probably read everything about baseball. For me, being interested in marketing is being interested in the marketplace, so my focus of reading and watching is to stay current on what's going on in the world. I'm always trying to make sense of it in terms of trends. I always try to put it together.

One of the traits I think you need to do this job, in addition to the skill of analysis, is the skill of synthesis. Analyzing is pulling apart. You have to be able to put things back together and to understand the trend. When I read those publications, I'm looking for trends. That's how I stay on top of what is going on. For me, it's about scanning the horizon for trends every day.

You get noticed by being part of an organization that succeeds, so you must surround yourself with very good people. You must work as a team member and do your job well. Lastly, you must have good judgment because the bets you make will be your success or failure.

Building a Successful Marketing Team

Putting together a great team is a must. You need people with the same passions, but with different backgrounds and experiences, so you get a broad view of the marketplace and the world. You have to enjoy interacting with people at all levels and want to understand what is going on in your world, or someone else's world. By the way, for a global company like ours, we do this internationally. It's not a matter of just the U.S. market, but also markets like Australia, Hong Kong, and Brazil. I look for a team of people who can help us understand other markets. It is so much easier to understand a culture where you have lived, as opposed to one where you haven't. We look for people who have the same love and understanding of the marketplace.

Next, I look for people who can synthesize many things down to a single-minded idea or thought. Third, I look for people who take an idea and instantly want to make it better, as opposed to dismissing it. There are two kinds of people. There are people who look at an idea and say it's horrible and dismiss it, and there are others who might not love an idea immediately, but who will work to make it better. I look for the latter. That requires curiosity. The last thing I would say is courage. Advertising and marketing are public endeavors, so you need the courage to deal with criticism.

The Importance of Setting Goals and Planning

As you can see from the steps I've discussed, setting goals is critical. When the goal is not well defined, you find the group-correcting course many times late in the project. This is costly from a dollar and morale standpoint. I am a big believer in clear goals. Knowing what they are is extremely important. Knowing where we're going is extremely important

The second piece of this is discipline. I think it is a mistake to believe that creativity does not require discipline. Some people believe that creativity is random. There is a random aspect to it, since it's not linear in process. I don't want to confuse discipline with linear thinking. What we do is not necessarily linear. I think marketing is part analysis and part inspiration. Inspiration can work with discipline. It requires the right input, having the right understanding, and then giving yourself some room to try things and think big. This still has to reside in a very disciplined organization and process.

The Future of Marketing

The unfortunate fall-off we have seen in the dot-com world further underscores the importance of marketing and branding. The more capitalism is successful in the world today, the more we are going to see branding and marketing be very pervasive tools, skills, and careers. Based on what I hear in the marketplace, there is a shortage of good marketers and branding people. There is a great divide between the people who theorize about branding and marketing and those who actually do it. There are many things written about the principles of marketing, but marketing is nothing if the principles aren't executed.

The proliferation of products and complexity of the population have caused marketing to become more sophisticated and to grow in importance. Branding has proved itself, in terms of the intangible value that it provides the company on the street, as well as in the points of sale. That importance has been recognized. I think branding and marketing will continue to be key skills that will grow in sophistication. The future will be very interesting. If you look at the Internet as an industry, I think it needs branding and marketing to succeed. It needs to understand how to charge fees for things it was giving away. All of those things are going to become more and more important.

John Hayes is executive vice president of Global Advertising and Brand Management, a position he assumed in May 1995. He is responsible for brand management and advertising across American Express. John manages the company's advertising agencies and oversees creative development, media strategy, and brand research. He is also a member of the American Express Global Management Team.

Prior to joining American Express, John was president of Lowe & Partners/SMS. In that position, he helped Diet Coke reverse its market share decline and the 35-year-old Sprite brand achieve double-digit growth. He also has held senior positions at Geer DuBois, Ammirati & Puris, and Saatchi & Saatchi Compton. He has developed advertising campaigns for Citibank, Aetna, Prudential Insurance, RJR Nabisco, Jaguar and Reebok.

John is vice chairman of the Association of National Advertisers and is a member of the board of The Tiger Woods Foundation. He received a BA in Marketing and Communications from Seton Hall University.

.

MARLBORO FRIDAY: BRANDING A PRODUCT

RICHARD RIVERS

Unilever

Senior Vice President, Home & Personal Care Division

The Brand Is Dead …

2nd April 1993 – "Marlboro Friday." Not a lot happened that day. In fact, the only thing that happened was an announcement from Philip Morris that it was cutting the price of a packet of cigarettes by 20 percent. But that was enough.

Stock prices fell off the edge of a cliff. Heinz, Quaker Oats, Coca-Cola, Pepsico, Procter & Gamble, RJR Nabisco, and all quoted advertising stocks plunged wildly – with Philip Morris itself being the hardest hit. There was genuine panic on Wall Street – and way, way beyond.

Looking back, why was it that so many experts, with such market influence, had so little faith in the resilience of established brands? The answer has important lessons for all those in the business of building and nourishing brands. Look carefully at most of what is written about brands – it becomes clear that, at heart, most experts and commentators believe that the art of branding is little more than an immensely clever technique for persuading consumers to pay more for their goods and services than any rational person should.

Some argue that brand values are first artificially constructed, then imposed from above on a gullible consuming public. In this view of the world, brands certainly have a real value, but only to their owners, never their users. The art of branding is a black art – a means of persuading the innocent to part with large sums of money in return for something called "image" which has no material usefulness at all.

The markets admire this greatly, of course, because it makes money. But they fear it, too, because of its obvious fragility. Some day, inevitably, the consuming public will come to its collective senses; rationality will return; choice will once again become based solely on price; and the age of the brand will be over for good.

With these largely unspoken assumptions as background, it becomes a great deal easier to understand Marlboro Friday. If the whole branding business is such a con-trick, at some point the whole thing is bound to come crashing down to earth. The moment one manufacturer significantly cuts the price of one of its brands, hysteria erupts – just like what happened on that fated Marlboro Friday.

The Power of Brand!

There were, of course, a great many people who, though astonished by the rhetoric, remained staunchly unmoved. And just as the actions of those who panicked were driven by ignorance, so the actions of those who didn't panic were driven by knowledge. They understood a fundamental truth: Brands exist because people want them to exist. Even if the word "marketing" had never been invented, and advertising was banned across the globe, there would still be brands, because it is people who need them.

Branding is a natural, instinctive, human creation – a way of making a complicated world simpler. With a brand, you get a symbol, a cue – you know what you're getting, what to expect. When William Lever first cut bars of soap into regular-sized pieces, wrapped them, and added the name Sunlight, he added accountability – the first step in consumer protection. Put a name on a product – brand that product – and yes, there's a guarantee of consistency. If you like what you've bought, you know you can buy it again and again. Yet just as importantly, from the consumer's point of view, there's now someone to blame if there's anything wrong. If you don't like what you've bought, you know what to avoid – and what to tell your friends to avoid.

Many social commentators seem to believe that brands are mainly for the relatively affluent – for those who choose to pay a little more for the insubstantial pleasures of fashion or style. Yet take a look at history – or at today's developing markets – and it's clearly not the case.

Among the first to appreciate William Lever's Sunlight soap were those who had so little money that there was no such thing as a trivial purchase. Any mistake was a serious mistake. Sunlight saved them from painful error. That guarantee of "satisfaction … or your money back" wasn't an expensive one because, of course, every bar of Sunlight was just the same as the one you bought before. In Rajasthan, the Unilever brand of soap, Lifebuoy, is eagerly bought by the poorest people there. Why? Because the much cheaper alternative is an unmarked product sold by the scoop from an oil-drum. At the very lowest income levels, paying a little more for a guarantee of quality, safety, and consistency makes enormous sense.

So it is people who call brands into existence, who form attachments, detest homogeneity, value consistency, and delight in conferring personality characteristics on animals, entities, and inanimate objects. People have been confidently differentiating between objects since they were first invited to make a choice between two identical arrowheads. Schools, universities, and football clubs have brand values. Cities, streets, and even postcodes have brand values. And perhaps the most compelling example of all is the brand value we attach to every individual human being. To date at least, there's been no multi-billion-dollar advertising campaign designed to make the population of the world find each other desirable – they seem to do it quite instinctively!

We should never forget what is so often misunderstood: A brand – unlike the product it contains – is created by, is valued by, and lives exclusively in the mind of its consumers.

Where Brands Go Wrong

On reading his own premature obituary, Mark Twain sent a telegram to the Associated Press with the dry comment: "The reports of my death are greatly exaggerated." Looking back on the panic of Marlboro Friday almost a decade later, much the same could be said for the death of brands. Yet if this is so, why do so many brands decline and die? If brands in general are so resilient, why are individual brands seemingly so vulnerable?

The reason is that companies kill them – not normally deliberately or knowingly, but through negligence or neglect. They're always sad when it happens, but seldom surprised. The death is often so lingering and so protracted, that it takes on the appearance of inevitability. But as some brands have demonstrated, there is nothing inevitable or predetermined about brand decline.

Why Established Brands Die

There are a number of reasons brands die, and I want to

focus on five of the most common: arrogance, greed, complacency, inconsistency, and myopia.

Arrogance

How do you kill a brand by arrogance? Quite simply, you forget the fundamental truth about brands: Ultimately, they belong to consumers. You persuade yourself that brands belong to brand managers and forget what it was that made the brand useful to the consumer in the first place. You lose sight of the fact that it is consumers, not companies, who invest a brand with its value. Lose sight of this, and companies start imposing values on a brand that are incompatible with those that matter to the consumer. Inevitably, brands start to lose their coherence – and nothing wounds a brand more than incoherence. Consumers love brands for their consistency. Deny them consistency, and they're soon drifting away by the thousands.

A prime way of achieving this incoherence is through an endless cycle of relaunches, upgrades, and brand extensions. Unleash on the market such a proliferation of brands, with virtually no functional features or personality to distinguish them, and soon even the most discriminating consumer is unable to tell one from the other. This sort of brand proliferation has all the subtlety of the blanket bombing techniques perfected in the last war, and it simply leaves consumers dazed and confused. Research suggests that 90 percent of new product launches fail – I find it astonishing that 10 percent succeed in our crowded market.

Over 70 years, Unilever has built up its business in practically every country around the globe. As a result, it is perhaps not surprising that the company has ended up with a vast portfolio of brands. Equally, that is no way to ensure that those brands best serve their consumers. That is why we are currently embarked on a strategy of streamlining and focusing our brand portfolio: to ensure that we can invest in building our strongest brands – those brands with greatest consumer appeal – rather than dissipating energy and resources on brands with limited appeal or potential.

What's important is staying connected with individual consumers, and then innovating to meet their evolving needs, rather than confusing them with unnecessary complexity. We want our brands to be favorites – first in the market, sometimes second, but not fifth, sixth, or seventh – because big brands can innovate and grow for their consumers.

Greed

Over the years, plenty of brands have been destroyed by creeping greed. Numerous companies have sought to make their prized assets more and more profitable, only to wake up one day to discover that they've pushed prices so far, or tampered to such an extent, that they've killed the goose that laid the golden eggs. Taking cost out of a product formulation sounds like an efficient thing to do – and sometimes it is. But more often it's the most effective way to starve a brand to death. We're not talking about dramatic, overnight reductions in standards or delivery, but shaving – a thin slice here, another in six months, a third by the end of the year. Each reduction is so insignificant that no one will notice – except, of course, people do notice eventually – and they always will.

An example of this phenomenon occurred with a range of Unilever soups, Country Soups, which was once performing badly in the marketplace. We agreed we needed to offer better value: to improve the quality of the ingredients and put in lots of chunky vegetables. Out of curiosity, we looked into the history of the brand to see what standards had been set for its recipe over the previous ten years.

What we discovered, perhaps not surprisingly, is that the wonderful, new quality standards we'd just agreed to, and all those chunky new vegetables, were almost exactly the same as those enjoyed by the brand ten years earlier. Then, little by little, brand manager by brand manager, those quality standards had been shaved away. Needless to say, the hope that this would go undetected and that margins would subsequently improve had proved a false hope. But we learned from the experience. When the price/value equation of a brand gets out of line, sooner or later – and usually sooner – people will notice. And when they do, they will act.

There, of course, lies the real lesson of Marlboro Friday. It was another case of creeping greed. Bit by bit, over time, hoping to go unnoticed, they got their price/value equation out of line. Yet more and more people sensed it; more and more people started drifting away; and Philip Morris' correction came just in time.

Complacency

The story is a familiar one. A company or brand builds a good reputation, sits back, and rests on that reputation, only to wake up one day to discover that faster, hungrier, more innovative competitors have passed them by. IBM is a good example, not least because it's a company that, since feeling the pain, has successfully reinvented itself.

The sequence of events goes like this. To begin with, you are, for example, a very technologically advanced company – and deservedly very successful. As the market becomes more and more competitive, you realize that you need both product performance and brand character to stay ahead. Brilliantly, you build a great image for the brand, so that users not only respect the company, but feel loyal to it, as well. You grow even more successful.

Then comes the critical stage. You become such an enthusiast for the notion of brand personality – and become so fixated with your own – that you come to believe that competitive product performance is no longer your highest priority. So you neglect to innovate; you neglect to invest in R&D; you stop listening intently for those faint murmurs of discontent – and for a month or two, or even a year or two, your success continues, and your profits mount. You may even be tempted to believe that you have discovered the secret of perpetual motion.

Then, with savage suddenness, your once healthy brand becomes an invalid, losing share and reputation with precipitate speed. What has happened? Your market has discovered what you have done, and suddenly realized a once-loved brand has taken its users for granted. The response of its users is brutally unforgiving.

What happened to a computer company has happened to car manufacturers, to retailers, to banks, and to fast-moving consumer goods companies. Complacency is one of the easiest ways to bring a brand to its knees.

Inconsistency

Like arrogance, greed, and complacency, inconsistency is a tried and tested way to undermine a brand's consumer appeal. A brand is, after all, a trust-mark. It is useful to consumers precisely because it provides a consistent guarantee of quality. What is interesting today is that consumers' expectations of consistency extend well beyond the quality of the ingredients they expect to find in a branded product, or the customer service standards they expect from a branded service. Increasingly, consumers expect the values of a brand to be reflected in every aspect of the business behind the brand.

It may have been possible, not so long ago, for a brand to live a life securely ring-fenced from its corporate owners. Few members of the public knew the name of its manufacturer; even fewer allowed their view of that manufacturer to affect their view of the brand. Today, no brand enjoys such immunity. Naomi Klein's book *No Logo,* while misunderstanding the fundamental relationship between brands and their users, is nonetheless an important book for everyone in the brand business, because it draws attention to consumers' growing interest in the company behind the brand. It is easy to dismiss this as the activism of a handful of pressure groups with easy access to the Internet, who take a keen interest in how a brand is made, where it is made, by whom, how much they are paid, the conditions in which they work, how old they are, and how their wage relates to the price of the product they produce. It is easy – but also a mistake.

Today companies have nowhere to hide. Employees, consumers, governments, suppliers, shareholders, and the media not only take an increasing interest in every aspect of a company's activities, they also have the means at their fingertips to find out everything about them.

There is no more certain way to damage your brands than to be seen to have double standards. If there is not clear congruity between brand values and corporate values, both will suffer irreversibly. This has important implications for brand management. With the reputation of the entire corporation increasingly impinging on the reputation of every brand – and vice-versa – the responsibility for the management of brand reputation lies at least as heavily with the chief executive as with the company's brand managers.

Myopia

We live in a world of permanent change. Indeed, as has been said many times before, ours is a world in which the only constant is change itself. Change inevitably brings both challenges and opportunities. Those who fail to understand the consequences of change for their brands inevitably put those brands at risk. This becomes obvious once you consider the dramatic changes in brand communication in recent years.

The traditional image of brand communication is a strictly one-way affair: The marketing company tells the consumer good things about the brand; the consumer accepts this information gratefully and expresses that gratitude by buying the brand for the rest of time. The medium for the message is network television – and mass investment in mass-market advertising reaches a mass audience, which responds with satisfying obedience. This, of course, is a highly simplistic image. Even one-way communication has always contained an important element of consumer participation. Consumers will challenge, interpret, dispute, modify, or reject brand messages with great confidence.

That said, however, over recent years the rules of the game have changed beyond recognition. The fragmentation of media channels, the explosive growth of the Internet, and the changing attitudes of consumers have all chipped away at the 30-second network TV spot as the prime medium for brand communication.

What's more, the way in which consumers form their opinions of brands is increasingly complex. Companies may distinguish between main media, promotions, public relations, sponsorship, product placement, and the Internet, but consumers and potential consumers make no such distinction. To them, every brand encounter helps to build up a mental picture of the brand – whether it's a planned and paid-for piece of brand communication or a chance encounter of a different kind. They may read disturbing reports of a company in the newspaper, see its trucks being badly driven on the highway, be infuriated by incomprehensible instruction leaflets, be driven mad by the company's call center, or receive graceless and misspelled letters from home office. Each of these encounters has the potential to inflict serious harm on a brand's reputation.

If a company is unable to understand these changes in the nature of brand communication and the implications of every brand encounter, its brand will increasingly feel the consequences. In a world of rapid, constant change, myopia is a very dangerous state of mind.

Getting it Right

Companies, then, don't normally kill off healthy brands deliberately. But through arrogance, greed, complacency, inconsistency, or myopia, it is very easy to see how it happens all the time. This is not an inevitable occurrence. Other brands not only survive, but grow from strength to strength. Why do they survive while others fail? What do they get right?

There are plenty of opinions about this, the holy grail of marketing. But in my view, based on my experience with Unilever over the last 30 years, three factors stand out as critical foundations for success: powerful consumer insight, intense focus, and top-quality innovation.

The first key to success is to know, understand, and anticipate your consumers. Just as arrogance is so often the death of a brand, so deep, insightful consumer connection is key to the success of a brand. Behind every star brand is a powerful understanding of the brand's consumers – of why they value the brand, of how it meets their needs, of how their attitudes are changing, of how their needs are likely to evolve in the future. This understanding is the key to maintaining the brand's fundamental usefulness, even as tastes and needs, attitudes and desires evolve. And as the pace of changes increases all around us, so the ability to anticipate trends and lead change grows in importance.

Let me give you an example. Three years ago, at Unilever, we embarked on our own Foresight exercise, led by a team of young managers drawn together from around the world. They spent a year together, going round the world, meeting people, exploring the dynamics of change in our world, and mapping out how consumer tastes, needs, and attitudes are evolving. This insight has been immensely valuable to us, not just in responding to our consumers today, but in anticipating what they are likely to be seeking in five, ten, 15 years. That understanding and our ability to respond to it effectively will determine whether many of our brands prosper or decline in the years ahead.

Second, focus. Lack of focus means that energy and resources are dissipated. Focus, in contrast, ensures that time, people, and resources are concentrated where they can add greatest value.

I have already mentioned Unilever's current attempts to focus on a smaller number of powerful brands. This will mean that, instead of trying to drive growth through four or five brands in a particular category, we will focus on one or two – the ones that already have strong consumer appeal and real potential for future growth. Instead of fragmenting resources, we are able to invest in significant brand development and big-hit innovation for one or two. We are already seeing the consequences in the performance of our leading brands.

Finally, innovation. Successful brands retain their usefulness to consumers – but that doesn't mean they can afford to stand still. They must constantly evolve, and adapt to changes in consumer needs and aspirations. The driver of innovation is not just insight, but foresight.

Innovation that "tinkers" with a brand's functionality is masquerading as innovation – a new flavor here, a new pack design there, a "new, improved formula" that brings no improved consumer benefit. These innovations, valuable as they might sometimes be in terms of short-term revenue, can easily take on their own momentum, creating enormous consumer confusion, but adding little of value. In the long run, tinkering does nothing to expand a market and runs all the risks of the greed or complacency that I described earlier.

True innovation pushes the boundaries of markets in new directions. Look at some of ours: Lynx/Axe, the insight that propelled the brand to leadership came from the direct involvement of the 16-year-olds for whom it was intended; Flora was already well positioned as a heart health brand before "pro-activ" moved it to the next level of actually improving heart health; Dove expanded to embrace a wider range of products without losing its brand focus.

In anticipating consumers' expectations, these innovations greeted consumers with the new products and services they desired. They enabled the brands to stay contemporary and fresh while retaining the enduring quality that made them useful in the first place. These are the ingredients of brand survival and success.

Valuing a Brand

So we know why brands in general are so enduring; we have seen why some brands decline and die; we have looked briefly at what leads them to survive and prosper. Does any of this make it is easier to answer the question posed by Marlboro Friday: How do you put a value on a brand?

The truth, as Marlboro Friday and other similar moments have demonstrated, is that few investors would claim to have a real understanding of the nature of brands, or to have a rational approach to putting a value on them.

For a while, for example, dot-com brands attracted absurd valuations, even though most were manifestly not brands at all. Then the mood abruptly changed. First we were told that the coming of e-commerce meant the end of brands. Then an over-correction of sanity spelled the end for e-commerce. Ignorance leads not only to irrational exuberance, but also to irrational depression – sometimes both in the course of the same week.

The truth, of course, is that just about every social and economic change favors the strong and established brand. Retail brands did not replace the Heinz, Kellogg's, or Liptons. Nor will dot-coms replace the retailers. Strong brands are strong brands, whether they are detergents, motorcars, supermarkets, or electronic channels. The weak may shine brightly for a while – then fade and die. Indeed, as the whole world becomes more complicated, strong brands – as an essential piece of simplification for the consumer – are set to become stronger still.

As to valuing brands, fashions in business models may come and go – but cash flow remains a trusty and constant yardstick. The allegiance that a consumer feels towards a favorite brand – the predisposition to purchase that's built on a better product and a more useful bundle of benefits – is a capital asset. It is a reservoir, if you like, of future cash flow. The size of the reservoir depends on the distinctiveness, the relevance – at the end of the day, the fundamental usefulness – of the brand to the consumer, and then on the ability of management to keep the reservoir topped up with relevant innovation and flowing freely. This is what determines the value of the brand to its legal owners, and this is the value that ought to be reflected in the market.

Final Thoughts

What the new economy has very usefully done is remind us of the essential nature of brands – and just why the strong ones are so valued by their users.

Brands exist because people want them to exist. Though owned in law by companies, they are in every other sense the property of people.

There is no need for brands to die. "Cause of death" on a brand's death certificate should usually read "arrogance," "greed," or "complacency."

Old economy or new, brand principles are identical. Understand and honor them – and win. Shrug them off as yesterday's romantic nonsense – and you will certainly lose.

To function at all, human societies rely on the existence of trust. Good brands invite trust, earn trust, honor trust, and reward trust. Good brands guard their reputations with their lives; and if by accident they transgress, they apologize with grace and true humility – quickly.

Every change that we face in marketing today makes the establishment of trust and the maintenance of trust more necessary and more valuable because, for consumers, the mounting complexities of choice will make the need for trust more urgent. It is a promising future for brands that live up to and deliver on these expectations.

Richard Rivers is considered by many, both internally and externally, to be one of Unilever's most knowledgeable consumer brand marketers. He has actively participated in the creation of the Unilever Marketing Academy, which is responsible for the development of best practices in advanced brand communications around the Unilever world.

PROVIDING CHOICE

RICHARD COSTELLO

General Electric

Manager-Corporate Marketing Communication

Exciting Aspects of Marketing

The most exciting aspects of marketing, for me, are understanding the psychology and motivation of consumers and then positioning a product to appeal to them in a way that makes them either want to buy it or spend more on it. It is really the psychology behind it, getting inside the customer's mind and then doing something creative that persuasively speaks to them, whether it is a package, Web site, or advertisement.

Changes in Marketing in the Past Few Years

The techniques have changed, but the fundamentals haven't. In other words, you still have to figure out what people are thinking and looking for. The way you deliver that now is more diverse than before. Twenty years ago a television commercial was probably the primary way to communicate, followed by print, to a lesser degree. Today there are sponsorships, Web sites, email, place-based media, and a variety of other techniques.

The other thing that has changed is that there is more choice for the customer ... more brands, more features, and more options. This creates a battle for attention in the media on the shelf and in the consumer's mind. The consumer has also gotten smarter and is better informed than 20 years ago. The consumer is noticeably better informed, pickier, and more interested in examining their choices.

Impact on the Market by Dot-coms

The dot-com impact has been minimal. The reason for this is they are either dead or on their last legs. I would say if the proliferation that we saw in 1999 and 2000 had actually sustained itself, marketing would have been a real challenge. As it is, pets.com has gone under, and a lot of the grocery delivery systems are going under, as well as a lot of the retail delivery businesses. They are evaporating as fast as they proliferated. eBay looks to me like a survivor; AOL was already around. There are not a lot of survivors there. Brick and mortar brands are now using the Internet as another delivery system. For example, in the grocery distribution service, my sense is that Peapod and Netgrocer are going to disappear. But Kroger online may develop as a good way for the customer to order groceries if they don't have time to visit their local store.

Lessons to be Learned from Dot-coms

I think it is very difficult to build a brand instantly. The belief that you can run 50 million dollars' worth of ads and become a fully-fledged brand is naïve. Great brands deliver on a promise that fulfills a specific and real need. When I say deliver, I mean it really can do what it says it can. A lot of the dot-coms were over-promising. There were a lot of dot-coms that did what they said, but once the customers tried them, they decided that they didn't want them. How many people really need to be able to buy their pet food over the Internet? Not many. The final problem is that most of these companies didn't have any economic model that made sense. Pet food is a low-margin business. If a dot-com offers to deliver pet food to your home, it has to either absorb the delivery cost by reducing already low margins or charge a premium to the customer, which reduces the appeal from the consumer point of view. Either way, you have a business model that is not economic.

Changes in the Future of Building and Sustaining Brands

There are a number of ways to look at expected changes. First, I think from the point of the view of the brand promise to the customer, there will be an increasing need for narrowness of target and customization. I am not sure that any products will ever go down to one-to-one, but I do think that any brand is going to have to deliver very narrowly targeted products to small subgroups of people. Any manufacturer is going to have to deliver in many different formats, as well as types, to satisfy different people. You are going to have lots of niche products under an umbrella, satisfying a multiplicity of unique and different needs. This is true in virtually every product line. The key driver is the need to provide choice to satisfy a lot of consumers. This creates two challenges. First, marketers have to figure out what the needs of their consumer are and provide for them before the competition does. Second, manufactures must provide a multitude of different types, styles, and flavors at a low cost, which will be a challenge to the manufacturing part of the organization.

The second issue is there is going to be a huge proliferation in ways of reaching people, as there has been recently. In some ways, this makes marketing better, because there are lots of ways to choose from. But it also makes it worse, because by definition that means that there are going to be smaller and smaller audiences. Putting together plans and programs to reach the numbers of people that you need to reach to sustain a product line is going to become increasingly complicated. The challenge is managing an ever-increasing choice of marketing options … selecting among the Internet, magazines, whether or not you participate in sports marketing – if so, which sport and how will you advertise, what television programs you are going to use across a 500-channel environment and so on. There is a complexity here that we have never dealt with and that even now we are struggling with. It is just going to get a lot more complicated.

There aren't as many single-formula mass products as there used to be; instead, most successful brands evolve into many different varieties to appeal to sub-segments. There was a great article in the *Wall Street Journal* about Stove Top stuffing, which is a pretty basic product that has been around since the 1970s. The way they have survived and thrived is that they keep on coming out with new versions that keep the appeal of Stove Top fresh. That's one example of a classic, mass-market product adapting to new competitive challenges by proliferating its offering.

Building an Established Brand

The first component of building an established brand is a promise that is compelling. It is often simple and generic. Let me give you some examples of enduring brands: Coca-Cola, whose basic promise has been refreshment. This is a promise that is simple, compelling, and has been achieved. Disney promises family entertainment. Marlboro promises satisfaction and a macho, outdoors stereotype. Although they weren't first to take this approach, they have been the most effective and have been able to establish a pretty unassailable position. It is nice to have a unique promise, such as Apple's promise of friendliness to the customer, which is the niche they have taken. Not many people have competed with them in that area. All of the examples are simple and compelling … it is what distinguishes great brands.

The second component is delivering on that promise. When you pick up a Coca-Cola, you get the refreshment of bubbly, fizzy water with a shot of sugar and caffeine. That has delivered refreshment to people every time they take a hit of it. Marlboros deliver great, satisfying cigarette taste to those who smoke; Apple delivers user friendliness; Disney delivers family entertainment. Disney's promise is so well established that they can't release an R-rated movie under the Disney brand because it would undermine their entire image. Disney does this under other labels such as Touchstone and Hollywood Pictures. Disney has done maybe one or two PG-13 movies, ever. They understand their promise must be kept … they cannot afford to surprise or disappoint their audience.

The third component is consistency – consistency in the way you communicate your promise over time and consistency in presentation of packaging, environment, and design. The look, feel, and experience have to consistently reinforce the promise you have made, whether the consumer is in the retail environment or sitting in front of a computer screen. The more consistent you are over a period of time, the more effective and cost efficient you are.

An example in the appliance business is Maytag, a competitor of GE's. Maytag has used the symbol of the lonely repairman for 30-plus years. Their advertising has rarely won any awards, but is has been effective in establishing Maytag as a reliable brand that doesn't need repairing. They figured out that reliability of appliance is very important to consumers. The symbol of the lonely repairman communicates reliability to their customers. If you ask people what is the most reliable dishwasher, most people will say a Maytag, and that's a great example of effective branding. They have made a promise, stuck with it for 30 years, and positioned themselves very effectively. We know this because we compete against them.

That concept of consistency also can be demonstrated by Marlboro: It was originally targeted toward women, and it bombed because at that time women were infrequent smokers, and the heavy smokers were men. It shifted to the now familiar cowboy imagery in the early 50s, and that turned the brand around. I have seen the original cowboy ad in black and white, and it looks virtually identical to today's ads. The only difference is that they are now in color. But it is still Marlboro, and the brand promise has been consistent for 50 years now. Great brands do that.

GE has been making a promise for close to a hundred years that our technology will give you better living. I can show you ads from 1916 that demonstrate how people's lives were improved by using our technology in washing machines, irons, etc. It's a very generic promise of better living, and as early home innovators, we are able to own that simple idea. Over time, our promise has stayed the same. In the 1940s and 1950s our slogan was "Live better electrically," so it was the same idea. Now our slogan is "We bring good things to life." We have played down the electrical aspect now, but the idea remains the same. So over a long period of time, the focus has been on the lifestyle benefits that people get by using our technology rather than the technology itself. That's been a consistent positioning. Those things – consistency of communication, delivery of promise, and a powerful promise that is appealing to a consumer that may or may not be unique – are all important to building a brand.

Difficulty in Maintaining Consistency

It is going to be more difficult to maintain consistency, but people who have been doing it all this time and are good at it will figure out new ways. I think it is going to require more discipline and care, but if you have an underlying brand concept and a disciplined system of touch-point presentation, you should be able to pull it off. I think that the only brands that are going to survive long-term will build the appropriate internal processes to maintain their consistency.

Killing an Established Brand

Several things kill an established brand. The first is that the promise made becomes irrelevant. The product or distribution method becomes redundant, and the company doesn't shift to a new technology or way of delivering it. An example is a buggy whip manufacturer who had a great brand, but buggy whips died because no one used buggies anymore.

The second way is non-delivery of the promise. That could be for a variety of reasons. A great example is airlines when they reposition themselves. There used to be an airline on the East Coast called Allegheny. They changed their name to USAir and repainted all their planes. I remember the first time I got in one of their planes because inside they were identical, and they were as awful as ever. That's an example of a brand that did a re-branding that didn't succeed very well because they didn't deliver anything other than a paint job. If it is the same lousy airline, it doesn't matter what you rename it. If you make a promise and break it or imply something and don't deliver it, you are going to run into trouble.

The third way to kill a brand is if someone else comes along and does it better. A great example of that is Dell moving into the personal computer space and eating Compaq alive. The reason is not that they produce a better product, but they do provide a better way to shop. You can shop at home on the Internet or by catalogue, rather than experience the confusion of a computer superstore. You also can customize the product to your exact specifications. Delivery is fast, and the packaging and installations are easy and non-technical. This combination of convenience, customization, and user-friendliness has been hard for competitors to match. A competitive displacement happens when another guy comes in and does a better job.

Favorite Marketing Tools (High Budget)

First of all I love 60-second commercials because they are short enough to discipline you but long enough to communicate the promise. They are really a luxury that not many people can afford these days. They can be quite powerful. In magazines, I love gatefold techniques where you can make your brand really look big and exciting.

I also love direct mail that is highly targeted to a very specific group for a category that does not traditionally use this technique. You don't expect to see direct mail for the automotive category; it's not a catalogue or a credit card. I got a series of mailings from Mercedes for their new SUV when they were introducing it. I am not sure why they picked on me – I couldn't figure it out – but they did a beautiful series of mailings that intrigued me and caused me to go look at it, so I guess it worked! I thought this was a very effective technique.

Another great thing to do when you have a great product is sampling. It doesn't matter whether it is a 50-cent drink or an automobile for a test drive. Sampling is often very expensive, but it's a powerful mechanism if you have a great product.

Another technique in the business-to-business world is to do a seminar or some form of forum where you invite customers and prospects and provide them with value-added information. If you are targeting a small-business customer, doing a seminar for a day on how to make their small business more productive is a great way of connecting and capturing a relationship with them. That's almost the equivalent of sampling, but it's different because you don't actually give them the product; you just show them that you are an expert in their segment of business and provide them with valued information that predisposes them to let your salesmen come in and visit them. That can be expensive and tricky to execute, but if you do it well, it is very powerful.

Favorite Marketing Tools (Low Budget)

PR is probably the first low-budget favorite marketing tool. It is hard to do because you can't control it, but if you come up with a clever gimmick or idea, it is effective. For companies that have a physical presence in the community, that presence can be a great mechanism for marketing. A good example of this is U-Haul. They use their trucks as billboards to advertise their product. If you look at the truck, it has a big visual on the side that is very eye-catching, with different states featured on it. If you look more closely, it points out that there is a special low-step loading and shows the 800 number. It is selling you by just driving on the road. In the retail environment, there is very little paid marketing. They use the physical store and signs to sell the store; this is particularly true of an outfit like Starbucks. It has done very little advertising, considering its size and growth. Its stores are both its service and its marketing.

Budget Needed to Create an Established Brand

I don't think anyone knows what it takes to create an established brand. In the packaged goods area, there are models and formulas, and in that environment they might be accurate. But no one knows. It will vary by product type and the situation that product is in. Starbucks was able to build a brand with virtually no advertising because they had actual retail, visible presence, which acted as a billboard for them, as well as word of mouth through the type of product they had. You have the Gillette launch of the Mach Three, where they spent more than 100 million dollars, and it was very successful. So there are two opposite sides of the spectrum that are both very successful. Frankly, it's hard for me to come up with little guys. An example might be the flavored drinks such as So Be and Arizona, which relied more on word of mouth, given the uniqueness of their product, and which started in small local markets and spread out without heavy promotion. It's all over the map. I wish I knew – I'd be rich!

Innovation in the Market

For long-term success, innovation is critical. To sustain yourself over time and to keep interest and freshness, it is very important. A good example is computers. Michael Dell was able to break through the retail category by providing a different way of buying, and that was their innovation. He built a whole manufacturing distribution infrastructure that got around the traditional way of doing things. The other innovation in that category was Apple, which innovated through design, style, and interface, all being friendly and human. They are unique and distinct, too, but their success level is lower. These are two different ways of approaching a category, both innovative and both successful.

The automotive industry has been able to increase pricing of cars by constantly innovating, particularly at the high end. Adding in safety features, such as front and side airbags and antilock brakes, is an example of their innovation. The car is still fundamental – it still has four wheels and an engine – but by adding in innovations like that, they have been able to sustain pricing and avoid commoditization. Every three to five years a lot of them restyle their look, whether it is Mercedes, Jaguar, or Ford. They keep doing that to keep people's attention. Innovation causes people to take a second look.

Gillette's game has been to incrementally improve the shaving experience over time and keep the price up. They started with a single blade, then made a double blade and charged a bit more, changed to an aloe strip, and continually made innovations up to a third blade. Now a four-pack of razors is six dollars – I used to pay half of that.

Interestingly, they always keep the older products on the shelf, so that if the consumer is satisfied with an older technology or cannot afford the newest one, they are able to keep using what they have always used. This is a great example of innovating but remembering that not every customer is an early adopter.

The Importance of Reinvention for a Brand Name

I think you have to be true to your basic promise and constantly refresh the features. Let's look at Disney. Disney is family entertainment. It started off as cartoons in 1930. When television came around, they added children's entertainment with Disney shows on Sunday. Then they proliferated the brand to an experience by building the first theme park. When that worked, they added a more parks. As they built the parks, they kept refreshing them inside with new and more innovative attractions. Now they have a ship that you can go on for a Disney cruise. They also have hundreds of stores in malls. It is a combination of innovation and broadening the touch points for contact that the consumer may have.

Disney is constantly innovating, but the common theme is that it's for the consumer's family. Their theme parks are high-quality and clean, and they're a good environment for kids. So is every other product … stores, cruise ships, and movies. They have the old constants like Mickey Mouse and Snow White but constantly introduce new experiences, such as the theme park with real animals down in Florida. They keep coming up with new ideas to keep you there, spending more money and coming back more often, but the basic underlying theme is the same. Great brands do both at the same time: Keep their fundamental promise very much in mind, but think of hundreds of different ways of delivering that promise to you. It is this that keeps the brand fresh and exciting. A great brand is a paradox … on one hand delivering a singular, consistent promise and on the other a constantly changing series of diverse innovations and variations on the basic theme.

The Difficulty in Maintaining Innovation

I don't think maintaining innovation will be more difficult in the future. As technology advances and disposable income increases, it actually opens up more proliferation opportunities. I don't think that is as big a problem. The real issue is whether or not you can make them economically viable. An example of proliferation of a brand that was an economic disaster was for Marlboro. They have a direct-marketing arm that sells smokers Marlboro paraphernalia such as t-shirts, hats, and other such items. This is a way for them to build up a database of their smokers. They knew that bans on advertising were coming, and they were aggressively building a database so they could market directly to their smokers. They then decided to go into experiences and do an old-fashioned train and invited smokers to take a trip to the West. It was a disaster. It cost them a fortune to build this train; it never quite worked; and nobody got a trip. It's an example of how they were trying to innovate in their marketing techniques and were not able to pull it off. You can always come up with proliferation ideas; the questions are whether they are viable and whether they fit with your economic model. It turns out that train rides are not within Marlboro's business model.

Investment Results in Marketing

Ultimately you have to look at the P & L of the component parts of your brand and the amount of marketing expense in each of these component pieces. For a brand that is a single product – say for example, Tide, which is just detergent – the linkage of expense to that product line and the relative return is easy to measure in the sense that they might have spent $50 million, and the share might have increased one point. They can figure out whether or not this was a good return. The complexity comes when you have a brand spread out over numerous P & Ls. So you have IBM or Disney, which are mega brands that are spread out over a multiplicity of product lines. Here it becomes much more difficult to figure out what is working and for what reason. When IBM or GE does advertising about the company rather than about a specific product, it becomes much tougher to measure. Although customer perceptions might be enhanced for GE or IBM, it is difficult to link this effect to a specific transaction. In those cases, it is tough to measure effectiveness. You can measure things like perception of different attributes or feelings toward a company. You can often see them shift as you change marketing tactics. Getting that back to a bottom-line payoff is more difficult. In many cases it is more assumptive, and there is no direct correlation. Even in traditional package goods, these correlations are often difficult to get directly. I am wrestling with the question of whether or not we should spend $25 million on broad corporate advertising or $5 million each on five different specific products. That's almost impossible to get a definitive answer on.

Advantages of the Internet

I think that for business-to-business marketing the Internet is a fantastic tool. In most business-to-business relationships, you know the customer: Who she is, where she is, and what she is buying. Also, the transactions are often high-value. In those cases you can use the Internet to build extranets that provide a lot of value for the customer, as well as incentives. For example, in our medical systems business, we are selling MRIs that cost a million dollars or more to hospitals and radiologists. We can afford to provide all sorts of services on the Internet, such as monitoring the performance of the device minute-by-minute and being able to send them a warning when the machine is out of sync and sending a service technician before it actually goes down. These sorts of things are incredibly valuable to our customers, and we couldn't do them five years ago. The Internet provides the opportunity to build a much deeper relationship with our customers by connecting directly to them and providing value-added services.

Another example, GE Plastics: For our customers who use plastic in bulk, we use the Internet to monitor sensors in their silos to determine when they need a new shipment. We can send out a trainload of plastic pellets to automatically replenish a silo, so the customer doesn't even have to re-order it. These are just some of the amazing things that can be done in the business-to-business world.

In the consumer area, for certain products that are rich in information, such as cars and appliances, the Internet is a great means to provide people with information, so that they can make better decisions. I think that it's more difficult in the consumer market to leverage as much as you can in the business-to-business market, because you have a much more dispersed and less sophisticated audience that is difficult to identify. The Internet is a double-edged sword because the information it provides is very useful for the supplier and for the user, but it can also give the user information that was not previously available, such as comparative pricing. It definitely makes it easier for the customer to compare features and get a low price, so it creates pricing pressure in the marketplace. This has not happened in all categories, but it has in cars. It is interesting because people go the traditional route to the showroom, look at the cars, and get the brochures. Then they go home, get on the Internet, and shop for the lowest price. The consumer is much more informed and they use that to get buying leverage against the dealer. As a result, the dealer has to sell the car at a lower price because the customer is smarter. However, the dealer still has to keep the showroom and the cars because the customer is going to want to see the car and take a test-drive. So the dealer hasn't gotten rid of any cost, but the customers are walking in smarter and more price-savvy.

Bricks and Mortar Companies

I think there is a mental barrier for the managers of bricks and mortar companies. A lot of managers are confused and intimidated by the Internet. It took GE a while to get over that barrier. The dawning of the Internet age was 1995, and we didn't get our act together and go full forward until 1999, four years later. Once you get over that and say that you are going to do this, you have significant advantages over competitors not involved in the Internet.

The Internet requires three things: a great brand, a fulfillment mechanism, and an understanding of how to use Internet technology. The dot-coms have one of those: the smart, young kids who know how to do the Internet piece – but most of them don't have a brand or infrastructure of manufacturing or distribution and have to spend a fortune to build a brand and infrastructure.

For example take online grocery retailers. They had the net savvy, but they didn't have distribution, so they had to spend huge amounts of capital to build a distribution system and advertising to build awareness. The bricks and mortar grocers are at an advantage. They have a brand, and they own a distribution system. They only have to invest in the Internet technology. For example, Barnes and Noble had the bookstores and the warehouses to distribute the books. They had already done all this investment; now all they have to do is get net savvy and adapt their systems to it. That's all GE has done. Where we direct-sell to customers, the Internet enhances that relationship. What you have to do is get the organization to embrace the Internet and not be afraid of it.

It gets tricky for a manufacturer when they have a distribution system that relies on traditional bricks-and-mortar retailers, and they decide they want to go direct to the consumer. This puts the manufacturer in chief competition with their retailers. We partner with our retailers; we allow consumers to purchase appliances on our Web site, but pricing and delivery are executed by a local retailer they choose. As distributors get savvy, they will be the ones who continue to control the relationship with the end user. Wal Mart is going to have a great Web site, as well as great stores, and consumers will go to either place, and goods will be distributed in both places – electronically, as well as in bricks-and-mortar stores. That is how this is going to settle down. The jury is still out on whether Amazon can survive as a non-bricks-and-mortar brand.

Pitfalls to Avoid in Marketing

The first pitfall is to make a promise you can't deliver on. If you disappoint people, they never come back, and this can be catastrophic for a business. It is one thing to come up with great advertising that promises something really great, such as adding years to your life. If it doesn't deliver, then you are in deep trouble. I think that is a major problem that people have. Second, it is really easy to get seduced into spending enormous amounts of money on unproductive activity that has little or no return. You see companies spending huge amounts of money on sports marketing programs or special events where the linkage between the product and the activity is so remote that you have no understanding as to why they are doing this. It is really easy to get seduced into something nifty that is also expensive and irrelevant to the brand. I see a lot of that.

A brand sponsoring the Olympics is a great example. The U.S. Postal Service was a worldwide Olympic sponsor. I couldn't figure out what relevance it had to anything. After one Olympics and $50 million, they stopped doing it. I guess they figured it out, too. Another example is these cars racing around the NASCAR circuits. You wonder what the

199

logo is doing flying around on that car. Maybe the manager or the boss wants to go to NASCAR races for free, or rationalize that they can take valued customers to their races. However, most of it is ridiculous. Another good example is all of those dot-coms that put their logos on the Super Bowl games – this was an ego trip. Ego trips are fun, but they are a total waste of money. Stockholders should make citizen's arrests on these people. If I were a stockholder in some of these companies, I would go ballistic about what they were spending my capital on. At the Super Bowl, the dot-coms poured investors' money down a hole. Those are traps to avoid.

Unique Aspects of GE

The GE brand is one of the top ten brands in the world. It is that way because of its longevity and continuity. It has been delivering on the promise of a better life for a century. There are not many brands that have been around that long. People have an incredible emotional connection with it. It is in people's homes, in one of the most important rooms of the house, the kitchen: The refrigerator, stove, dishwasher, etc. These products nurture and feed people in a place where they gather and chat. There is a strong emotional connection to a traditional brand that is in this special place with them.

We are also reliable, and we don't let people down. We have good warranties and service; if something goes wrong, our company will be around to take care of the customer. Those are strongly held beliefs among our consumers. As we have moved and proliferated into other businesses, we have held on to those beliefs and delivered on our promise. If you talk to our radiologists, they have an even higher opinion of us because they see the technology we use in our MRIs. When they buy an MRI, they have seen that we have great service and will fix it if something goes wrong and will always be there to provide support. We are GE and are as good as the bank. We won't go broke. There is a sense of safety and reliability, but also with a flavor of innovation – people see us as very competent. That's the GE brand. It has been built through a combination of real delivery of products and services to people. Time has reinforced the GE brand; we have been around so long, it makes people very comfortable.

Fifteen years ago, I was interested in modernizing the logo of the company … it had been used unchanged since 1896. We are a high-tech company today making jet engines and MRIs with a hundred-year-old logo. I did research among consumers and management, and we found that people rejected any change in our logo. People told us we were crazy because their grandmother had it in her kitchen. Radiologists told us we were crazy because they had been treating patients with scanners carrying that logo for 30 years. Our employees told us we were crazy to change; that logo had been on every paycheck of their working lives. That shows you how powerful the customer connection is with the brand.

Leaders

I respect consistency that I think you get from brands that stick with a promise over time, and I have named some of them: Marlboro, Maytag, Disney, IBM, and Apple. I also respect brands that are not fickle to trends and the latest fashion. Many marketers appear to like change just for the sake of changing. It is almost like the message changes with each new brand manager. As the brand managers move with more frequency in an organization, you see the campaign changing more frequently, usually for the worse. Great marketers don't allow that to happen. Institutions with something that works stick to it through generations of management. These great branding companies have the discipline and the power of a great branding promise that keep the company steady and focused. Clearly, if it isn't working, it should be changed. But in a lot of cases, things are changed long before they stop working. I admire companies that stick with it through extended periods of time.

Changes in Marketing Over the Next Five Years

Marketing will not change as much as people like to say it will. The basics will remain exactly the same. Come up with a compelling promise, and deliver on it. The techniques are proliferating and becoming more complicated, and that will necessitate more simplicity of message. Promising to make people's lives simpler will actually become a more compelling promise in itself in the products and services you provide. I think people are becoming overwhelmed in their lives by complexity.

Making things simpler to choose, shop for, and finance will be a very compelling promise and trend. Having said that, I think that the reality of the world is that the choices will increase. This is going to require more effort to cut through and piece together a program that gets noticed. It's going to get more complicated, but I don't think the fundamentals will change; it will be more the execution that becomes trickier.

Richard Costello joined GE in the summer of 1980. During the ensuing two decades, he worked closely with GE's former chairman, Jack Welch, to shape brand strategy and implement the company's brand-building programs. Accomplishments include development of the "We Bring Good Things to Life" advertising campaign. This award-winning campaign is one of the best recognized in the world today. Costello has been responsible for maintaining the quality and consistency of the company's advertising across every GE-branded division globally.

Before joining GE, Costello worked in the advertising agency business for 12 years. In 1968 he started his career in a small London-based agency buying media, then moved to McCann-Erickson London. There he spent four years in media planning for clients such as Exxon, Martini & Rossi, and Beecham. In 1973 he moved to the New York office of McCann and switched to account work. For the next seven years, he worked on advertising campaigns for Best Foods, Brown & Williamson, J & J, and Gillette.

Costello is on the Board of The Advertising Council, the Association of National Advertisers (ANA), and the Norwalk Education Foundation (NEF). He is a past Chairman of both the ANA and BPA boards and current President of NEF. He is a frequent speaker on branding issues at industry conferences.

TURNING A BRAND INTO A NATIONAL PASTIME

TIM BROSNAN
Major League Baseball
Executive Vice President Business

Marketing for a Major Sports League

What is the biggest difference between marketing for a major sports league and marketing for a traditional company? Product. Baseball is a game, an entertainment product that cannot be physically packaged and sold from a store shelf like a box of soap powder. When you sell services or packaged goods, elements such as packaging, product content, and relevant advertising can all help to move the sales needle. Consequently, there is a direct connection between your marketing decisions and their impact on your sales. That is why consumer goods marketing is very nearly a science. Your quantitative and qualitative research can determine where to go, what to do, and what the result will be.

Sports marketing is more art than science. Without a gut feel – an innate understanding of your product – you won't be able to comprehend why consumers respond as they do to what you are selling. Know-how alone isn't enough. At one time or another, each of the major leagues has hired product marketers who tried to marry the classic principles of packaged goods marketing to sports marketing concepts. All of these attempts failed, even though brilliant professionals implemented many of them. These people came from an environment where possessing a passion for the product was not a requisite for success.

That's not to say they were completely disconnected from their merchandise. They understood what they were selling, as well as who they were selling it to, and that was usually enough to launch a successful program. Sports marketing, however, requires an emotional commitment. You have to live, eat, and breathe it every day to have any chance of getting it right.

Baseball: The Game and the Brand

You must also set clear goals. Our objective at Major League Baseball remains constant from season to season. How can we take this great game to the next level? Before you can appreciate the challenge this represents, you should understand the difference between baseball the sport and Major League Baseball the brand.

On the field, Major League Baseball is this wonderful game played between members of the world's athletic elite. As people watch this spirited competition, they gradually form personal attachments to teams and players. That bond between the game and its fans is the critical factor in any success the Major League Baseball brand enjoys.

When I write about Major League Baseball in upper case, I am referring to the game's super brand, whose internationally known trademark is the red and blue silhouetted batter. The thirty major league clubs are, in effect, sub-brands, each with its own logo and trademarks.

Marketers cannot extract full value from this super brand or its subs unless they can associate the quality of the play on the field with the fans' affinity for their favorite teams or players. The success of any marketing campaign depends on the deep emotional connection people make when they hear the crack produced by bat meeting ball. Baseball, therefore, must remain focused on its grassroots. Our research reveals that if people participate in a sport as children, they are more likely to follow that sport as they mature. So you can see why it is in our interests to encourage youngsters to play baseball, softball, stickball, punch ball, or any of baseball's other derivatives.

For years, we ignored that base. Now, however, we are aggressively courting young potential fans whose allegiance might otherwise be lost to other major sports, with a number of programs such as Reviving Baseball in Inner Cities (RBI) and the Diamond Skills competitions. These are, of course, in addition to our financial support of the many youth Baseball programs, such as Little League. The aim is to introduce boys and girls to baseball early to help develop their preferences. Our efforts are not confined to the U.S. alone. Bringing "stick and ball" games to children all over the globe is vital for the game's future.

Imprinting the Game

Imprinting the game presents a formidable challenge for any sports marketer. It also raises a philosophical question: Can you have a business without a sport? Our answer is no. True, the business alone may capture people's fascination, but only for a short time. For instance, when the NFL tried to enter Europe in the 1980s with the likes of Joe Montana and William "The Refrigerator" Perry, Europeans were immediately attracted by the game's gladiator-like spectacle and its larger-than-life participants. Sales of NFL merchandise boomed in these virgin markets. But since there were no ongoing games aside from the occasional special event to sustain the interest – no actual sport or league for the fans to regularly connect with – that business quickly contracted. With no one putting kids into helmets and shoulder pads and teaching them how to play football, there was no way to nurture any long-lasting interest in the sport.

Soccer offers us a similar example. I used to drive out to Giants Stadium to watch the Cosmos play Major League Soccer. I wanted to see Georgie Best, Mario Chinaglia, and the ultra-charismatic Pele perform because they were international personalities who were considered the best in their field. I didn't play soccer; in fact, I knew next to nothing about the game. But I was attracted by soccer's superstars, so the sport held my interest – for about two years. Then the thrill evaporated for me, as well as many others. The Cosmos folded, and the business, Major League Soccer, died. Teams could not sustain themselves because they had not developed the underlying sport. They had failed to imprint it in the minds and DNA of American fans.

This brings us to a critical advantage that Major League Baseball enjoys over all other sports, as well as other forms of entertainment – its identity as an American cultural institution. They call it "America's Pastime" for a reason. If you ask Americans to identify their first sporting experience, most will say it was a baseball game they attended with their dad or family. Or they will vividly recount their first physical contact with the sport, that first hit or diving catch. And we all know fans who can't start their day until they peruse the latest box scores over breakfast.

Many of us mark time by our baseball experiences. I remember the last big San Francisco earthquake occurred in 1989 because it interrupted the World Series played that year between the Oakland A's and the San Francisco Giants. And when you mention 1998 to an American, he or she is more likely to recall Sammy Sosa's and Mark McGwire's pursuit of Roger Maris's single-season home run record than Bill Clinton's impeachment hearings.

With the game so deeply ingrained in their psyches, the American people believe that they own Major League Baseball, and they're right. As marketers, we are responsible for making sure our consumers continue to feel this deep attachment to the game. At the same time, we must also discover the means of exporting that attachment abroad, while preserving the game's cultural identity.

To bring any sport to the next level, a marketer must recognize what the next level is. As I said earlier, at Major League Baseball, our goal is to create greater participation and global reach. Attaining that objective requires us to "grow" the game up from the youngest levels. I'm not just talking about attracting new fans. To ensure that Major League Baseball is sustained as a business, we must build the game player by player. If we can persuade more children to play baseball around the world, the talent pool teams have to draw from will expand. Yes, some of them might not leave their country to play the game here. But many of them will. Only recently, a young Russian player – a six-foot, nine-inch pitcher – was quoted in the *New York Times* saying, "If you want to be a baseball player, you have to be in Major League Baseball." That sentiment is not uncommon, and it confirms how human nature compels us to gravitate toward testing ourselves against the best.

That young man's words underscore a simple idea. The more people participate in baseball, the more likely it is that the best form of baseball, *i.e.,* Major League Baseball, will flourish. This, above all else, should be the primary objective for any sport and its super brand: to capture your audience, your target market, early on. Everything else is subordinate to that goal. However, the challenge of marketing baseball is further complicated by other considerations.

Competition With Other Forms of Entertainment

Baseball is fighting for the consumer's entertainment dollars. Contrary to what some die-hards may believe, our game is not a staple. If you did not have Major League Baseball, your life might be less enjoyable, but you would not starve. Any money fans spend on the game and its products is discretionary. Fortunately, most people consider entertainment to be an important part of their lives. They are willing to invest time and money in any activity that promises nothing more than sheer enjoyment. But that discretionary income is limited. So baseball is not only competing with other major league sports for those dollars, but we are also competing with every form of entertainment, from rock concerts to movies to CD-ROMs.

My children have an infinitely more diverse variety of entertainment choices than I ever had growing up. I would run out of the house after school and play baseball until dusk eight months out of every year. My friends and I did not have the Internet or numerous television channels, rinks, learning centers, DVDs, and video games to distract us from the ball field. Baseball's most obvious competition comes from other sports, but we must never forget that we are competing with every form of entertainment.

The Role of the MLB Brand

As the super brand, Major League Baseball should never compete with its sub brands. Instead, Major League Baseball must authenticate and support the club brands. It cannot do that unless we protect the super brand at all cost, to make sure the quality of the sport it represents never diminishes. When consumers see that Major League Baseball trademark, they should immediately associate it with the game at its best, the premier form of baseball competition in the world.

As we simultaneously extend the reach of the super brand and its subs, we must guarantee that our logos and trademarks stand for high quality and value. Our licensed consumer products not only generate revenue, but they also provide us with an excellent barometer of baseball's appeal to the general public. When someone buys a product licensed by Major League Baseball, it carries either our brand, the silhouetted batter, or one of our club marks. The purchaser is making a personal decision to display their affinity with their favorite sport, team, or player.

We want to make that sale because it means the consumer will leave the store carrying our flag. But it would be foolish to make that sale at all cost. We can't just slap our marks on some low-cost, shoddily made item, simply because it will move from the shelves in vast numbers. All of our brands must represent goods of the highest quality wherever they are displayed.

A real danger exists whenever a sport makes the mistake of considering itself a "lifestyle" brand. The moment sports leagues began thinking that Tommy Hilfiger provided more direct competition for them than another sports brand, they started slapping logos on everything from Hawaiian shirts to jam shorts. While baseball has nothing against being fashionable, we stay away from fashion's cutting edge because it tends to be ephemeral. By the time the public has defined what's "in," it's often already on its way out. We also want the consumer's focus to remain on the MLB or club brand. It would prove ultimately counterproductive to transform their affinity for baseball or their favorite team to an affinity for Ralph Lauren or some other designer name.

The best models for baseball in this area come from Nike and ESPN. These sports brands have broadly extended their reach. Nike might be in jeopardy of making its brand so ubiquitous that it may cease to mean anything special. However, consumers still buy Nike not only because they think the swoosh icon looks cool, but because they think it stands for the best in sports equipment. And they buy ESPN because it represents the best in sports entertainment. Regardless of how Nike or ESPN positions its brand, its magazines, restaurants, or media programs, Nike and ESPN have been able to expand without losing their core. You can bet that is a continual challenge for them. Major League Baseball is prepared to meet that same challenge.

Athletes as Representatives for "The Brand"

There is a big difference between marketing a sport that features human beings interacting within it – the athletes – and marketing a manufactured consumer product. You may be able to manipulate, manage, control, and package the consumer product at your whim. You simply can't do that with athletes. Major League Baseball players are highly skilled performers, simply the best in the world at their craft. It is their spectacular play that attracts people to the sport.

Nevertheless, athletes are human and often fail. No marketer can control their play, which represents the core of our business. And the success of our marketing and branding efforts depends on their performances off the field, as well as on. The poise and grace Cal Ripken, Jr., demonstrated season after season while establishing his record for consecutive games played had an enormous positive impact on our business. The 1998 home run race waged between the effervescent Sammy Sosa and the Bunyanesque Mark McGwire – and the mutual respect these two athletes demonstrated to one another despite their competition – added luster to the Major League Baseball brand throughout the world. But while these players were becoming celebrated, other players were slumping or encountering problems off the field. Our job is to find a way to sell it all, the highs and the lows, to market the human element that lends this great game so much drama.

Dollars and Sense – Financial Goals

Major League Baseball is currently a three billion dollar enterprise. Baseball is a sport, a sacred cultural icon held by the team owners in the public trust. However, we must never forget that it is also a business, and, like any commercial undertaking, it exists to make a profit.

Staying mindful of our profit motives produces clarity. An advertising CEO I know holds an annual session for his new creative and account executives. The first question he asks at the meeting is, "Why are you here?" Every year, the answers are the same. People say they want "to create the best advertising in the world" or "to win a Clio Award." No one has ever told him that he or she wanted to make money for the clients, the agency, or its shareholders. But that's the right answer, and it in no way conflicts with their other goals.

When I pose the same question to our new staff members, I often hear, "We are here because we hold the game in the public interest and want to preserve the integrity of the sport." There's nothing wrong with that response; in fact, it neatly fits an important piece of Major League Baseball's mission. But the answer is incomplete. *Profit is a worthy priority.* Our 30 franchise owners – our stockholders in a very real sense – wish to enhance their asset values while increasing their cash flows, just like the owner of the corner grocery. We are here to help them do just that. The good news is that if we all act out of a genuine love of the game, we will inevitably do things that generate profits.

That Devil in the Details

Like any Fortune 50 company, Major League Baseball must address its core business issues. Just like AOL Time-

Warner or Microsoft, we have to know what our brand and products stand for, and we must understand our target audience. Among the questions we have to answer are:

What does the consumer like or dislike about our brand?

Why is someone drawn to our product?

What do they purchase and why?

How do we compare to our competitors?

What are our ultimate goals?

One of our business unit managers used to say, "If you don't know where you are going, any road will take you there." I believe that when you market any business, you must survey the present environment, consider any outside factors that may have an impact on your industry, then make a calculated decision about where the business should be five years hence. Only then can you draw up an appropriate plan to reach your objectives.

This Buck Doesn't Pass

Another critical element in marketing any business is accountability, to both management and your customers.

You must tell your various constituents what you are going to deliver, then deliver it on time and as promised. Sound simplistic? You bet, but many businesses suffer or fold when they fail to keep promises made to their customers or shareholders. If you are going to tell the public that your company considers service to be job one, you must make sure that your phones are answered courteously and your orders are shipped promptly. Otherwise, you and your product or service will lose all credibility.

Sports marketing can be a fuzzy business. You can't always measure a marketing program's value unless it makes an immediate, direct impact on the bottom line, and that isn't often the case. I tell our customers and constituents what our goals are so that it is easy for them to judge whether we performed up to the expectations we created. Once customers see that we have, they are usually satisfied and willing to give us the authority we require to do more.

How to Lead a Sports Marketing Organization

Before you can lead any sports marketing organization, you must understand that your employees represent your most valuable assets. They must be willing to work with you while matching your competitive drive. Shrinking violets need not apply. You want people who will not only respond well to any challenges you present, but who will also challenge you. They must be able to simultaneously compete with each other and support the greater good of the team. And, as I mentioned earlier, everyone on your team must love sports. They have to be fans.

As the leader, you must make sure each employee fulfills his or her role. At times, you will have to make tough decisions regarding a team member's competence and performance. If you cannot be straightforward and frank in your appraisal, if you can't bring yourself to jettison any slackers, you will lose your credibility with everyone.

Where We Are Going

Baseball is a service oriented business. Our fans will continually bring us new challenges. When some cutting-edge technology presents itself, we must exploit that technology by adapting new marketing strategies. We must be smart and nimble enough to expand with every opportunity.

Currently, our primary medium for marketing baseball is television. The 2001 All-Star Game gave us the opportunity to reach forty million consumers for three and a half hours. The FOX network has been a terrific television resource for Major League Baseball. During the first five years of the FOX/Major League Baseball partnership, the network captured a younger audience, which we have been able to target with great success. We are working closely with network executives and producers to formulate the best way to present our games without compromising the competition on the field. And we are excited about the vast marketing and broadcasting potential presented by the Internet.

Major League Baseball already has its share of international stars from El Duque to Ichiro. Next, the game itself must become truly global. As our fan base diversifies, baseball will benefit from increased revenues and larger talent pools. Exporting the game worldwide will undoubtedly mean that our marketing strategies will change. However, no matter how innovative we become, the game will remain unaltered. Major League Baseball is ultimately nine guys playing nine other guys for nine innings with three outs to a side. We can discuss presentation with our television partners and fiddle with a rule here and there to improve the game, but baseball will always be baseball. And that may be the best advantage we have.

Tim Brosnan was named Executive Vice President, Business in February 2000 and is one of four Executive Vice Presidents reporting directly to Major League Baseball President and COO Paul Beeston. In this role, Brosnan oversees all domestic and international business functions of the Major League Baseball central offices, including licensing, sponsorship, domestic and international broadcasting, special events, and MLB Productions.

Brosnan joined the Office of the Commissioner in 1991 as Vice President of International Business Affairs. He was promoted to Chief Operating Officer of Major League Baseball International in 1994 and to Senior Vice President, Domestic and International Properties in 1998.

Prior to joining Major League Baseball, Brosnan was appointed to the New York State Commission on Government Integrity by Governor Mario Cuomo in 1987 and two years later was appointed counsel to the Chairman for that Commission. In 1989, Brosnan was selected as a Regional Finalist for the White House Fellowships. He earned a BA from Georgetown University, where he was a four-year player and captain of the baseball team, and a JD from Fordham University School of Law, where he graduated as President of the Student Bar and Commencement Speaker. He began his career practicing law at the Park Avenue offices of Kelley Drye and Warren.

Brosnan is currently a member of the Board of Directors of the Fordham Law Alumni Association and several of its fundraising arms. Brosnan also serves on the Board of Directors of the Baseball Tomorrow Fund. He is a member of the New York City Bar Association Sports Law Committee and is a founder and Board Member of the De la Salle Academy, a private non-profit school for underprivileged, gifted children.

ASPATORE MARKETING REVIEW
Tear Out This Page and Mail or Fax To:

Aspatore Books, PO Box 883, Bedford, MA 01730
Or Fax To (617) 249-1970

Name:

Email:

Shipping Address:

City: State: Zip:

Billing Address:

City: State: Zip:

Phone:

Lock in at the Current Rates Today-Rates Increase Every Year
Please Check the Desired Length Subscription:

1 Year ($1,090) _____   2 Years (Save 10%-$1,962) _____
5 Years (Save 20%-$4,360) _____   10 Years (Save 30%-$7,630) _____
Lifetime Subscription ($24,980) _____

(If mailing in a check you can skip this section but please read fine print below and sign below)
Credit Card Type (Visa & Mastercard & Amex):

Credit Card Number:

Expiration Date:

Signature:

Would you like us to automatically bill your credit card at the end of your subscription so there is no discontinuity in service? (You can still cancel your subscription at any point before the renewal date.) Please circle: Yes   No

*(Please note the billing address much match the address on file with your credit card company exactly)

Terms & Conditions - We shall send a confirmation receipt to your email address. If ordering from Massachusetts, please add 5% sales tax on the order (not including shipping and handling). If ordering from outside of the US, an additional $51.95 per year will be charged for shipping and handling costs. All issues are paperback and will be shipped as soon as they become available. Sorry, no returns or refunds at any point unless automatic billing is selected, at which point you may cancel at any time before your subscription is renewed (no funds shall be returned however for the period currently subscribed to). Issues that are not already published will be shipped upon publication date. Publication dates are subject to delay-please allow 1-2 weeks for delivery of first issue. If a new issue is not coming out for another month, the issue from the previous quarter will be sent for the first issue. For the most up to date information on publication dates and availability please visit www.Aspatore.com.

in the world on ways to master the art of deal making. These highly acclaimed deal makers from companies such as Prudential, Credite Suisse First Boston, Barclays, Hogan & Hartson, Proskaur Rose, AT&T and others explain the secrets behind keeping your deal skills sharp, negotiations, working with your team, meetings schedules and environment, deal parameters and other important topics. A must have for every financial professional, lawyer, business development professional, CEO, entrepreneur and individual involved in deal making in any environment and at every level.

Inside the Minds: Chief Technology Officers (ISBN: 1587620081)

Industry Experts Reveal the Secrets to Developing, Implementing, and Capitalizing on the Best Technologies in the World - *Inside the Minds: Chief Technology Officers* features leading technology executives from companies such as Engage, Datek, Symantec, Verisign, Vignette, WebMD, SONICblue, Kana Communications, Flooz.com and The Motley Fool. Their experiences, advice, and research provide an unprecedented look at the various strategies involved with developing, implementing, and capitalizing on the best technologies in the world for companies of every size and in every industry.

Inside the Minds: The Wireless Industry (ISBN: 1587620200)

Industry Leaders Discuss the Future of the Wireless Revolution - *Inside the Minds: The Wireless Industry* features leading CEOs from companies such as AT & T Wireless, Omnisky, Wildblue, AirPrime, Digital Wireless, Aperto Networks, Air2Web, LGC Wireless, Arraycomm, Informio and Extenta. Items discussed include the future of the wireless industry, wireless devices, killer-apps in the wireless industry, the international landscape, government issues and more.

Inside the Minds: Leading Women (ISBN: 1587620197)

What it Takes for Women to Succeed and Have it All in the 21St Century - *Inside the Minds: Leading Women* features CEOs and executives from companies such as Prudential, Women's Financial Network, SiliconSalley.com, Barclays Global Investors, RealEco.com, AgentArts, Kovair, MsMoney.com, LevelEdge and AudioBasket. These highly acclaimed women explain how to balance personal and professional lives, set goals, network, start a new company, learn the right skills for career advancement and more.

Inside the Minds: Venture Capitalists (ISBN: 1587620014)

Inside the High Stakes and Fast Paced World of Venture Capital - *Inside the Minds: Venture Capitalists* features leading partners from Softbank, ICG, Sequoia Capital, CMGI, New Enterprise Associates, Bertelsmann Ventures, TA Associates, Kestrel Venture Management, Blue Rock Capital, Novak Biddle Venture Partners, Mid-Atlantic Venture Funds, Safeguard Scientific, Divine interVentures, and Boston Capital Ventures. Learn how some of the best minds behind the Internet revolution value companies, assess business models, and identify opportunities in the marketplace.

Inside the Minds: Leading Consultants (ISBN: 1587620596)

Industry Leaders Share Their Knowledge on the Future of the Consulting Profession and Industry - *Inside the Minds: Leading Consultants* features leading CEOs/Managing Partners from some of the world's largest consulting companies. These industry leaders share their knowledge on the future of the consulting industry, being an effective team player, the everlasting effects of the Internet and technology, compensation, managing client relationships, motivating others, teamwork, the future of the consulting profession and other important topics.

Inside the Minds: Leading CEOs (ISBN: 1587620553)
Industry Leaders Share Their Knowledge on Management, Motivating Others, and Profiting in Any Economy - *Inside the Minds: Leading CEOs* features some of the biggest name, proven CEOs in the world. These highly acclaimed CEOs share their knowledge on management, the Internet and technology, client relationships, compensation, motivating others, building and sustaining a profitable business in any economy and making a difference at any level within an organization.

Inside the Minds: Internet Bigwigs (ISBN: 1587620103)
Industry Experts Forecast the Future of the Internet Economy (After the Shakedown) - *Inside the Minds: Internet Bigwigs* features a handful of the leading minds of the Internet and technology revolution. These individuals include executives from Excite (Founder), Beenz.com (CEO), Organic (CEO), Agency.com (Founder), Egghead (CEO), Credite Suisse First Boston (Internet Analyst), CIBC (Internet Analyst) and Sandbox.com. Items discussed include killer-apps for the 21st century, the stock market, emerging industries, international opportunities, and a plethora of other issues affecting anyone with a "vested interest" in the Internet and technology revolution.

Bigwig Briefs: Management & Leadership (ISBN: 1587620146)
Industry Experts Reveal the Secrets How to Get There, Stay There, and Empower Others That Work For You
Bigwig Briefs: Management & Leadership includes knowledge excerpts from some of the leading executives in the business world. These highly acclaimed executives explain how to break into higher ranks of management, how to become invaluable to your company, and how to empower your team to perform to their utmost potential.

Bigwig Briefs: The Golden Rules of the Internet Economy (After the Shakedown) (ISBN: 1587620138)
Industry Experts Reveal the Most Important Concepts From the First Phase of the Internet Economy
Bigwig Briefs: The Golden Rules of the Internet Economy includes knowledge excerpts from some of the leading business executives in the Internet and Technology industries. These highly acclaimed executives explain where the future of the Internet economy is heading, mistakes to avoid for companies of all sizes, and the keys to long term success.

Bigwig Briefs: Startups Keys to Success (ISBN: 1587620170)
Industry Experts Reveal the Secrets to Launching a Successful New Venture
Bigwig Briefs: Startups Keys to Success includes knowledge excerpts from some of the leading VCs, CEOs CFOs, CTOs and business executives in every industry. These highly acclaimed executives explain the secrets behind the financial, marketing, business development, legal, and technical aspects of starting a new venture.

Other Best Selling Business Books Include:

Inside the Minds: Leading Accountants
Inside the Minds: Leading CTOs
Inside the Minds: Leading Deal Makers
Inside the Minds: Leading Wall St. Investors
Inside the Minds: Leading Investment Bankers
Inside the Minds: Internet BizDev
Inside the Minds: Internet CFOs
Inside the Minds: Internet Lawyers
Inside the Minds: The New Health Care Industry
Inside the Minds: The Financial Services Industry
Inside the Minds: The Media Industry
Inside the Minds: The Real Estate Industry
Inside the Minds: The Automotive Industry
Inside the Minds: The Telecommunications Industry
Inside the Minds: The Semiconductor Industry
Bigwig Briefs: Term Sheets & Valuations
Bigwig Briefs: Venture Capital
Bigwig Briefs: Become a CEO
Bigwig Briefs: Become a CTO
Bigwig Briefs: Become a VP of BizDev
Bigwig Briefs: Become a CFO
Bigwig Briefs: Small Business Internet Advisor
Bigwig Briefs: Human Resources & Building a Winning Team
Bigwig Briefs: Career Options for Law School Students
Bigwig Briefs: Career Options for MBAs
Bigwig Briefs: Online Advertising
OneHourWiz: Becoming a Techie
OneHourWiz: Stock Options
OneHourWiz: Public Speaking
OneHourWiz: Making Your First Million
OneHourWiz: Internet Freelancing
OneHourWiz: Personal PR & Making a Name For Yourself
OneHourWiz: Landing Your First Job
OneHourWiz: Internet & Technology Careers (After the Shakedown)

Go to www.Aspatore.com for a
Complete List of Titles!

**ASPATORE
BOOKS**